Praise

M000278391

Stepping Into

An embodied approach to developing women leaders.

This book will invite you to travel to your inner 'self' through the fascinating stories of powerful women. Eunice's ability to embed her profound knowledge of somatics in the narrative of human journeys makes her methodology tangible and easy to access. While reading your heart will beat faster as each chapter will fuel you with inspiring moments.

Antonella Francabandera, Global Head of People Growth and
Talent Acquisition, Boehringer Ingelheim Pharma GmbH & Co. KG

A stirring and fascinating collection of stories from women that bring to life the true impact of finding your voice and stepping into your power. The stories strike a chord and are accompanied by punchy questions and invitations to reflect and practice. Be ready to be inspired, be provoked and be heard…

Emma Brock, Global Head of Organisational Effectiveness, Wavemaker

This book is about learning to be in tune with your physical presence, the profound connection between feeling and being, and a reminder that, as women, by having each other's back, we extend our own power. The stories I read reminded me of my own personal commitment to demonstrate that women can do great things, because when given the chance, they can truly do anything.

Valeria Della Rosa, Head of Client Services – Italy, ThoughtWorks

An inspiring and empowering read, *Stepping Into Your Power* is about discovering courage, aligning actions with purpose, and understanding what it truly means to lead authentically. This book beautifully brings together the choices these unique women have made, and from these choices, how they successfully spoke truth to power. What an amazing journey for the reader, who is taken through the lives of these authors and through each of their brave choices is able to learn how to step into their own power.

Sevana Melikian, Leader Development Manager, Cisco

Stepping into your power is a simple and powerful approach on what we women wish to see in the world. Six beautiful true stories of women who succeed in the corporate world, relating their challenges, drawbacks and how by listening deeply inside, were able to make the right choices, discover and understand their purpose, transform their identity by disrupting their embodied patterns to show up as themselves.

A must read for all women who support women, D&I supporters and all those who want to discover the power of your inner space.

Patricia Taparelli, Senior Manager, Leadership & Development, Sonova AG

Could the world be a better place if more women stepped into their power and were more present in the board rooms, at the helm of the governments as well as organisations that can make a real difference in our society? This is not a new question. And we all know the answer. However, why are we still asking ourselves this question? Why are we not living the actual experience of having more women in the leadership roles? Based on my own observations while dealing with women of all ages (from teenagers and university students to successful businesswomen and female policymakers), there are plenty of women who can make it. They can succeed. They can manage the others and lead effectively. But very few make it to the top. And often all it takes is to have someone to give them this confidence of stepping into their power. To show them the way, give them confidence that their dreams can come true. All it takes is to stop hesitating and start spreading your wings to fly away, to shine, to lead the others by example, to make this world a better place. If you are holding this book, it means that you are searching for answers, you are looking for the direction of travel. This book will help you. Will inspire you. Will show you that getting to a leadership role is not a challenge. The real challenge is to recognise and step into your power, be confident in communicating this to the others, be true to yourself at all times, and never forget to be humble and human, no matter how much power you can achieve in your future professional career.

Victoria Zinchuk, Director, Head of Croatia,
European Bank for Reconstruction and Development

Relatable, realistic and full of empathy, if ever you thought you were alone going through life experiences this great read illustrates how much we all share and can learn from one another. The practical advice and exercises at the end of each chapter allow you to go back time and time again to remind yourself of the combined power of body and mind… thank you, Eunice and co-authors, here's to remaining centred!

Pravina Ladva, Chief Digital Transformation Officer, Swiss Re Management Ltd

Aquilina's latest offering seamlessly blends wise commentary and potent embodiment practices with the sharing of her own and other female leaders' moving, honest and inspiring stories of accessing their power. It's a hugely timely and transformative book – one I wish I'd come across in the early years of my career and one I hope will fall into the hands of women leaders and their champions all over the world.

Liz Hall, Editor of Coaching at Work, Author of
Coach Your Team (Penguin, 2019), *Mindful Coaching* (Kogan Page, 2013)

Stepping Into Your Power is an invaluable guide for women in leadership positions who want to make a difference in the way they lead themselves and others. Eunice Aquilina shares the core elements of her life-changing somatic leadership coaching work in a compelling way together with powerful women she has guided so wisely and effectively on their path. This book is written in a real 'power-with' style: an outstanding coach and practitioner together with outstanding women leaders sharing their personal learning path and their vulnerabilities in an incredibly frank and open way. These women offer side by side guidance for women the world over who truly seek to bring their real power to life, and to their work.

Ute Nunnenmacher, Leadership Coach, pingworks – IT Consulting, Germany

Eunice will empower you with tools which can be drawn from at a moment's notice. These practices grant you the ability to recognise and manage through situational stress. Female leaders, if you're in search of your voice while leading through change, I truly recommend reading this book.

Aleah R. Titus, Operations Manager – Americas, ABB Traction

The soul-touching, candid personal stories transported me right into each writer's moments of realisation, personal learning and new-found ability to step into their power. This is the book to read this year for inspiration to unlock your personal power.

Carmen Drinkwater, Non-Executive Director,
Northern Care Alliance NHS Foundation Trust

In her quest to explore how we can 'begin to create organisations that work for everyone', Eunice combines rigour, action research, powerful personal narratives and great warmth to show us that 'power with' is the future. Whilst she focuses on the stories of women in workplaces shaped by archetypically male characteristics, the principles and practices of centred power are universal. The themes will resonate with anyone confined to a smaller, more manageable self by established structures and customs. Every reader will gain insight into the kind of personal development work that enables us to embody the full potentials of our humanity in our workplaces.

Amanda Ridings, author of *Weekly Leadership Conversations* and *Pause for Breath*

Stepping Into Your Power is an inspiring read, offering stories from real women leading change in organisations.

Murielle Maupoint, CEO, Play Action International

Stepping Into Your Power

An embodied approach to developing women leaders

Eunice Aquilina

Copyright © 2021 Eunice Aquilina

The moral right of the author has been asserted.

Apart from any fair dealing for the purposes of research or private study,
or criticism or review, as permitted under the Copyright, Designs and Patents
Act 1988, this publication may only be reproduced, stored or transmitted, in
any form or by any means, with the prior permission in writing of the
publishers, or in the case of reprographic reproduction in accordance with
the terms of licences issued by the Copyright Licensing Agency. Enquiries
concerning reproduction outside those terms should be sent to the publishers.

Matador
9 Priory Business Park,
Wistow Road, Kibworth Beauchamp,
Leicestershire. LE8 0RX
Tel: 0116 279 2299
Email: books@troubador.co.uk
Web: www.troubador.co.uk/matador
Twitter: @matadorbooks

ISBN 978 1800462 427

British Library Cataloguing in Publication Data.
A catalogue record for this book is available from the British Library.

Typeset in 12pt Minion Pro by Troubador Publishing Ltd, Leicester, UK

Matador is an imprint of Troubador Publishing Ltd

To Bernadette and all my young friends who took that journey to Valletta all those years ago; your strength and courage over the years has inspired me to find my voice and to step into my power.

In Gratitude

Throughout this journey, I've been supported, guided and challenged by friends and colleagues who at different times generously gave their time and energy. I've valued each and every conversation I've had and, in particular in those moments of self-doubt, being reminded to find my ground and reconnect to what was important. I want to take a moment to extend my deepest gratitude to all of those who've played a part in bringing this book to life.

First of all, to Maureen Silvester, friend and fellow somatic practitioner, who patiently read and re-read every draft, offering me her wise counsel from the early beginnings through to completion. The editorial insights she offered were invaluable, often leading to a radical re-write or even a complete re-think. Maureen continually encouraged me to own the value of what I was writing, inviting me to expand my vision for this book, by gently challenging me to go beyond my own limiting narrative. Thank you.

I also want to thank Kate McGuire, Liz Hall, Wendy Briner and Maxine Burrell who read later drafts of the book. Kate has been hugely supportive of *Stepping Into Your Power* and continues to be a valuable thinking partner. Her wise reflections really helped me broaden my ambitions for this work. Liz Hall, who did me the honour of bringing her editorial expertise to my completed manuscript, not only offered words of encouragement but also her incisive editing. I felt I was in safe hands. The clarity and guidance I received from Wendy Briner, my long-time supervisor, ensured rigour in my research, a strong theoretical underpinning and thoughtful application to practice. Maxine Burrell, who takes every opportunity to spread the word about my work with women, offered constructive editorial comments to the final manuscript.

I would also like to extend my gratitude to the team at Matador for their support and guidance through the publishing process.

This book has truly been a collaborative effort and I owe particular gratitude to my fellow scribes. It has been a privilege to work alongside them, inviting them to bring their unique voices to our collective endeavour; Fernanda Lopes Larsen, Carrie Birmingham, Alison Lazerwitz, Lucia Adams and Amy Castoro. Five amazing women who agreed to join me on this journey, giving generously of their time inside of their busy lives. Thank you. It was an honour to work with you all and to share the opportunity to bring such important wisdom to these uncertain times.

I've had the privilege of learning from so many extraordinary thought leaders and teachers in the field of organisation and leadership development, that it's only right to acknowledge some of them here as my work stands on their shoulders. My heartfelt thanks to Richard Strozzi-Heckler, Arawana Hayashi, Wendy

In Gratitude

Palmer, Staci K. Haines and Tiphani Palmer for waking me up
to the wisdom of my body. I also want to acknowledge Margaret
Wheatley, Mee Yan Cheung-Judge, Fernando Flores, Bill Torbert,
Julio Olalla, the late Michael Chender, Otto Scharmer, Toke
Paludan Moeller and the late Mike van Oudstshoorn. Thank you
for your work and your generosity in sharing it with the world.

To the extraordinary women I've had the privilege to work
with, thank you for putting your trust in me and for engaging so
fully in the learning; I've learned so much from each of you.

It's very often the people closest to us who are impacted the
most when we embark on writing a book, so last but certainly
not least I want to extend immense and deep gratitude to those
at home, my family. Their patience, unyielding support, love and
care made it possible for me to write this book. I feel so blessed,
thank you.

Contents

Foreword

It feels as if the world is unravelling. As I write this, we're in the midst of a global pandemic, with populations in lock-down and social distancing becoming part of our everyday lives. As we each learn to find our place in a world with COVID-19, we're beginning to entertain the idea that the world may never be the same again. Inside of this, voices in support of the Black Lives Matter movement are being heard. We're witnessing anti-racism protests in many of our major cities across the world, sparked by a variety of incidents, including the death of George Floyd who died in the street in Minneapolis under the knee of a police officer. People coming together, standing together, marching together – in support of racial justice and equality for all.

These are moments in history that are inviting us to put humanity first. We have an opportunity to deconstruct old patterns, to evaluate and re-evaluate what we truly care about, what really matters to us. A chance to pause, to centre and ask what this time may be asking us to pay attention to that we haven't been paying attention to before, becoming more fully open to what wants to emerge.

It's also a time when we're hearing more women's voices and seeing more women emerging as powerful role models inviting a different kind of leadership. We see that some of the countries that seem to be doing well in responding to the coronavirus crisis have women leaders. I'm not suggesting that in order to successfully navigate COVID-19 you have to be a woman as there are many male leaders doing great work too such as Emmanuel Macron[1]. However, given that women make up just 7% of heads of state[2], highlighting the contributions these women leaders are making helps other women see what's possible.

Many of these women leaders faced into the crisis early on, embodying an authentic presence, demonstrating empathy, speaking with care and compassion, and acknowledging their own self-doubt and feelings of vulnerability; leaders who are showing up as authentic in their power. Jacinda Ardern, prime minister of New Zealand, recently stated, "One of the criticisms I've faced over the years is that I'm not aggressive enough or assertive enough, or maybe somehow, because I'm empathetic, it means I'm weak. I totally rebel against that. I refuse to believe that you cannot be both compassionate and strong."[3]

This book brings together the voices of women leaders who embody their authentic power and who bring their voices to the world, making significant contributions towards a more inclusive workplace. While none of these women are leading a country, their voices are no less important as they too are role models for women leaders, showing what becomes possible when women speak their truth, their way.

As you read on, I invite you to breathe, to drop into your body and feel the call to be the leader and do the work of leadership as guided by your inner consciousness. I invite you to embrace your humanity.

Dr Eunice Aquilina Founder and Director of eaconsult
Author of *Embodying Authenticity*

Prologue

As we begin our journey, Deborah Whitworth-Hilton, Gas Storage Operations Manager for Uniper, offers us a short story of her experience of learning to step into her power.

"Walking into the Garden Room at Wasing Park to meet my fellow soon-to-be Embodied Leaders was both daunting and exciting at the same time, very much hoping that the next three days would guide me to understand and become a better leader. Whilst remaining open minded, I was also curious as to what this programme would bring me that I hadn't already seen and tried, but, oh my word, was I about to be blown away!

It might have been that this programme was at absolutely the right time for me both at work and in my personal life, or it might have been I was already en-route to the road of enlightenment. Wherever and whatever I was, being in this programme with my new-found family was totally life-changing.

Forever the engineering brain, believing that power came from knowledge and regularly over-thinking, to be encouraged to spend time attuning to our bodies, our feelings and sensations was completely liberating and beyond valuable.

I'd achieved my executive position as leader of a gas business in the UK, as a woman in a traditionally male environment, and proven myself as a supporter and active enabler of individuals' development, but something was missing. Something was restricting me from pushing me further. I'd thought that I'd always managed to hide my serious lack of confidence and self-doubt and this is something I hoped to explore and eliminate with the help of this programme.

From the invitation to make my initial declaration and the repeat of it on the second day, I soon realised that I wasn't being true to myself. How could I support others to be the best they can be if I'm not 'being' myself? Only by re-focussing my declaration did I give myself the permission to do things for me, to accept that I have a strong, colourful back that is full of a strong, colourful history, experiences, knowledge and skills that I should use to feel proud, be happy and have the confidence to just be me.

The strength I felt from relaxing my cognitive muscles and taking more notice of my feelings, emotions and somatic sensations, from realising and sharing my moods and origin story and from practising and appreciating centring and acknowledging my space, was so awakening. All of a sudden, the issues I brought to the course had dissolved. I felt lighter, confident in my abilities and reason for being and content in who I am – I left the programme as the real, genuine, powerful me.

With my revised declaration of living a fun and happy life for me very much at the front of my mind, the very next day, I took my first step on finding my own happiness – I ended a two-year relationship. It was nerve-wracking at the time but as I sat in the car on my journey home, the surge of strength I felt absolutely convinced me that I'd done the right thing and that my time was now. For the first time, I was being honest to myself, and not doing things just to please others.

This new-found confidence continues in the workplace where I allow my body to guide me, rather than over-think things, the results of which have been a more responsive and positive-thinking team. I'm a calmer leader, focusing on the things that matter, trusting my ability to lead a business and support people to be the best they can. At times of uncertainty, I take the time to centre and sense the way forward. On a personal level, I'm proactively pursuing my next career move rather than waiting to be asked – I have a lot to offer and am keen to share it.

I now realise and believe that power is not knowledge, aggression and high earning. Power is actually the strength you feel in yourself to show up as the genuine you, own your own space and presence in a team and lead your business, your team and yourself to the success you deserve."

Since writing this short story, Deborah has successfully been promoted to a global role; she is now Director of Operational Support for Uniper.

Introduction

The game's up

One of the dominant discourses in organisations today is around gender. The #MeToo movement has seen many women coming forward, telling their stories of how they've endured inappropriate behaviour in the workplace. Many of the reported cases in the press centred in and around Hollywood; however, the abuse stretched far beyond the film and entertainment industry with women coming forward from business, public service, and the Houses of Parliament. It has even affected a recent nomination to the Supreme Court in the United States as Christine Blasey Ford stepped forward to testify that Brett Kavanaugh had sexually assaulted her as a teenager.

At the same time, the inequality in pay across the UK suddenly took centre-stage as organisations with more than 250 employees were required to submit a report on pay levels across all their staff. The report revealed that eight out of ten companies pay their male employees more than their female employees, with more than a quarter continuing to pay women 20% less than men[4]. It's now nearly 40 years since equal pay legislation was passed into law in the UK and yet discussions on how to reduce the disparity between male and female pay are still prevalent in and outside of many boardrooms. Indeed the public sector broadcaster in the UK, the BBC, reported[5] a drop in its pay gap from 9.3% in 2017 to 6.7% in 2019 which is impressively low compared to the national average in the UK of 9.6% and the US of 19.3%.[6] However, despite the good work the BBC finds itself embarrassed by the inequalities that still exist. In early 2019, the Corporation hit the headlines when a female manager turned down the role of deputy editor in the BBC Radio newsroom after she discovered she was to be paid £12,000 less than a male colleague in the same role. Headlines like these serve as a reminder to us of just how embedded in our culture inequality is. There's still a long way to go.

Despite this, there's plenty of positive evidence building a case for having women in senior positions. According to McKinsey[7], companies across all sectors with the most women on their boards of directors significantly and consistently outperform those with no female representation – by 41% in terms of return on equity and by 56% in terms of operating results. This is backed up by a Catalyst report[8] on Fortune 500 companies revealing that those with the highest percentile of women on their boards outperform those in the lowest percentile by as much as a 53% higher return on equity, a 42% higher return on sales and a 66% higher return on invested capital. Even disregarding that women make 70% of the purchasing decisions in the EU, and 80% in the US, it's obvious that having women on boards makes sense economically.

Many companies have recognised the value of a more inclusive workforce and developed sophisticated talent management processes to increase the number of women being appointed to the board or to senior level roles, resulting in small improvements. Indeed, a report by Deloitte[9] suggests that women held 22.5% of board positions at Fortune 500 companies in 2018, up from 20.2% in 2016. Furthermore, women held 25% of board seats in Fortune 100 companies, which is an increase of 2% on the previous year.

However, while we may feel encouraged by the direction of travel, there is emerging recognition that having a robust talent management process in and of itself is not enough. As women seek to progress in their leadership careers, they can find themselves caught by the norms, belief structures and unconscious biases that continue to be inherent in so many of our workplaces. For example, women still bear the responsibility for the majority of work associated with children and running a home. Being assertive and decisive as a woman is often seen as bossy or bitchy[10]. Socialisation makes certain ways of being 'acceptable' for women but not for men. And all too often these factors lead to women either failing to reach their full potential or choosing to leave their job in favour of a 'better' work-life balance.

Those who stay may feel that they need to let go of what feels authentic to them, moulding themselves to be more like their male counterparts. I remember a client saying to me, "As a woman, I don't feel I can speak my truth in the workplace." So many women become adept at fitting in. And in the process, they lose the ability to articulate what they stand for, what their personal vision is, the impact they wish to make and the changes they want to bring about, casting doubt on their strategic capability. This leaves women who find themselves in powerful, influential positions battling to make their voices heard and struggling to use their power and influence in a way that honours who they are. The cost to organisations is immense, not to mention the price paid by the women themselves who frequently find other ways to use their talents outside of these corporate constraints.

Organisations often respond to these issues by reviewing structures, creating new processes, policies and procedures, offering awareness training and/or providing more knowledge – all of which are essential to creating a more equal workplace but are only part of the solution. If companies are serious about achieving gender equality and celebrating diversity in the workplace, they need to become aware of and more conscious of the social norms, the customs and practices that support and perpetuate inequality and start to understand the historical and social forces that have literally shaped us: our actions, reactions and our interactions. The pathway towards creating more inclusive organisations begins with leaders themselves, with stepping into their own developmental work, learning to interrupt their automatic reactive responses to access a more conscious, more resourceful, more choiceful self. By shifting some of our habitual ways of being, both individually and collectively, we can move beyond our history and the systems we've inherited and begin to create organisations that work for everyone. A more inclusive workplace invites women to show up in all their power, to take on more senior roles, and contribute more fully to the leadership of the organisation by bringing their voices to the table with impact.

There is a good deal of evidence to suggest that women-only spaces are more conducive to learning than mixed gender ones. Data from schools[11] indicates that girls perform better academically when they study in an all-female as opposed to a co-educational environment, while research into developing women leaders suggests that participants are more open and willing to be vulnerable when learning with other women[12]. I know from my own experience, and from working with other women, that the capacity to develop trust and nurture vulnerability, both key leadership skills, happens more readily when women come together without men.

However, learning, change and transformation don't happen in isolation so any intervention should also include activities that support the whole system, which obviously includes men and non-binary people too. In most organisations this means creating new leadership practices that support a more conscious, inclusive culture, where everyone can show up. As James Edgar, global chief talent officer at Wavemaker, shared with me, "it is like an organ transplant; the body, the whole system needs to adapt, or the new organ will be rejected." We cannot simply work with women on their own and then expect things to change when they slot back into the prevalent culture with its own shape and practices. The question becomes: 'how do we create a more inclusive culture where everyone can find their voice and where everyone can participate and contribute to the benefit of all?' So I am not talking about 'women's work' here – it's work for all of humanity.

Consider this old riddle:[13] a father and son are in a horrible car crash that kills the dad. The son is rushed to the hospital; just as he's about to go under the knife, the surgeon says, "I can't operate – that boy is my son!" If you guessed that the surgeon was in fact the boy's mother, then research[14] would suggest you're in the minority. Our social conditioning is such that we find it hard to imagine that the surgeon could actually be a woman. We cannot ignore that we still live in a white male-dominated culture which continues to shape our thinking and our automatic norms of behaviour. Moreover, Caroline Criado Perez, in her book *Invisible Women*[15] shares how the default to male is so woven into our everyday language that even gender-neutral terms are still likely to be interpreted as male. This default is in the very fabric of our lives and as such informs how we attribute meaning, how we construct identity as well as how we interpret power.

Our inherited definition of power tends to be one of 'power over',[16] a controlling power that perpetuates compliance and authority, re-enforcing hierarchy. It creates an environment where competing with each other is the norm and achieving the goal or delivering against some numerical target is the recipe for success. Creating organisations that work for everyone requires a shift in our interpretation of power from the prevailing 'power over' to 'power with' and a sense of the whole being greater than any one individual. It's a shift that invites a move away from the traditional organisational operating model of hierarchy and authority to leveraging the collective wisdom of the whole, moving from control held by the few to empowering the many. Equally it means accessing power within ourselves in order to build connection, vision and empowerment together. When we step into the truth of ourselves and we embody power, we can lift each other up and begin to change perceptions. As women, we have the responsibility to have each other's backs as we bravely step into being the change we wish to see in the world. As the American politician and diplomat Madeleine Albright famously said,[17] "there is a special place in hell for women who don't help other women."

As women, I believe we have a responsibility to bring our voices to the table in a way that creates change in the institutions we work for and the society, and perhaps most importantly, the families we live in. We're empowered to speak up, to call out the bad behaviour and to call on others, both men and women alike, to support us. "When women are able to step out from the shadows with their voices and their bodies then things start to shift. The gaps close.... It's time for women to be seen.[18]"

This book gives voice to some incredible women who are bravely stepping out of the shadows, letting themselves be heard and seen, and who are navigating their space in the world in new and different ways, achieving extraordinary results. I have had the privilege of working with each of these powerful women. I know their stories and I know the work that they have done. I acknowledge their courage, to step into their own vulnerability and speak their truth. From an early age we learn how to numb vulnerability, to contain or suppress the emotions we don't want to feel. We adopt emotional patterns that enable us to feel safe and to belong, emotional patterns that become embodied and shape the actions we want to take and the conversations we want to engage in. However, when we embrace our vulnerability, staying present to the inevitable fear that arrives, we allow ourselves to be seen.

Their stories weave together to create a rich tapestry; an invitation to you the reader to wander in and amongst, to reflect on your own relationship with power. Notice the voices you are drawn to, those that resonate with your own experience and those voices that inspire you or provoke a new interpretation of power for you.

In the course of my work, I have had the opportunity to engage with passionate, inspiring and intelligent women. As women leaders in different global organisations they often shared the challenge of navigating a culture that over-privileged the archetypal male. As part of my work, and in developing and evolving my own practice, I have engaged in action research[19] with over 100 senior women. This ongoing enquiry also enabled me to deepen my understanding of the relationship between embodiment and women's capacity to lead from a place of power and authenticity. I explored their lived experience of power, what gets privileged in which context, what this might mean for what gets co-created and how they show up in their leadership. I gathered their stories through one-to-one exploratory dialogues and action inquiry groups from which five key themes emerged. These themes underpin the stories my contributors have written, and I have included a brief summary of the relevant research at the end of each chapter. You may notice that some stories are expressed in US English, others in UK English, as a way of honouring contributors individual voices.

There is also an invitation at the end of each chapter, for you to pause and reflect on some questions or try a short-embodied practice as a taster of stepping into your power. I don't believe you can really experience this work through the written word alone, it has to be experienced with someone alongside you as your guide, but my hope is that the practices I have included will give you a flavour of the power of this work.

Our journey starts with my own story; moving from being afraid, keeping myself small, hoping not to be noticed to finding my voice, being able to hold the space for the conversations that matter, publishing a book and fully embodying being the CEO of a successful consultancy. Not letting my fear run me.

Let's begin…

Chapter One

Becoming

"Women endure entire lifetimes of these indignities—in the form of catcalls, groping, assault, oppression. These things injure us. They sap our strength. Some of the cuts are so small they're barely visible. Others are huge and gaping, leaving scars that never heal. Either way, they accumulate. We carry them everywhere, to and from school and work, at home while raising our children, at our places of worship, anytime we try to advance."

Michelle Obama, *Becoming*[20]

A call to action

It had been an extraordinary day, a day like no other. Along with many others from across the island I'd walked out from school – I'd gone on strike. I was just 12 years old and had courageously taken a stand for something I believed in; I'd stepped into my power.

1

A change of government on the island of Malta where I grew up had brought with it a fundamental reform of the educational system. One of the proposed changes was to reduce the length of the summer break in all secondary schools from three months to six weeks. In some countries this may seem quite a small thing, but it wasn't for us. The extreme heat of the summer months already made school in June unbearable. We often found it difficult to concentrate as the intense heat made the classrooms feel like ovens and with no air conditioning, students would even pass out. This controversial change to the summer holidays prompted outrage amongst the student population; it was the topic of conversation in every classroom in every school. Feelings were so strong that a call went out to all schools for students to come together and go on strike.

This was a time before social media, before emails, texts and mobile phones, so I'm not entirely sure how we co-ordinated with all the different schools. All I know is I'd arrived that morning to the news that today was the day we'd been talking about and waiting for, we were 'going on strike'. I remember feeling excited by the prospect and somewhat terrified too. I wasn't alone. We'd only been together as a class for a year and yet we felt strangely connected and united in our belief that this proposed change to the school holidays was unfair. As 12 noon approached, I looked around the classroom; we were all looking nervously at each other. I'm sure if we had been able to talk, we would all have asked the same question; did we really dare to do this? But as the clock chimed, quietly and determinedly we each put down our pens, closed our books, put away our belongings and silently walked out of class.

The silence was broken once we joined other students in the playground. The 'plan' was to walk out of school and make our way to the capital city of Valletta where we would meet students from other schools and march to the parliament building. Suddenly and quite spontaneously this sea of green and lemon uniforms began to move out of the school – only to be stopped by the headmistress, Miss Azzopardi. I can't recall exactly what she said to us but I'm pretty sure that the message was one of "do this and your academic life will be over." This was coming from the same woman who on the first day of school said to us all, "you are here for an education but make no mistake, your role in life is to get married, look after your husband and have children." So rather than deterring us, the headmistress' words made us more determined to leave. Some of our fellow students did think again and returned to the school, but I, together with my friends Vicky, Mary and Josette, kept walking. We were headed for the capital and nothing was going to stop us.

However, word had got out that waves of students were making their way to the capital. The police had been called in and were now positioned at all the bus stops. We decided to start walking so we could find a bus stop where there was no police presence. Before we got too far the police caught up with us, aiming to put us on a bus which would take us back home. However, in all the confusion we managed to evade them and got ourselves on a bus that took us to Valletta.

Arriving in the capital city, we made our way to Kingsway, known today as Republic Street. We met with students from other schools across the island and chatted enthusiastically. An observer may have thought that we'd already won our cause, but no, we were just feeling victorious and energised in our endeavours. By chance I managed to meet up with my friend and neighbour Bernadette and her school friends. They'd been able to walk into the city from their school avoiding having to get past the police. Together, as one student group we began to walk to parliament making our protest against the proposed changes. I was struck by just how much more powerful we became as we came together as one student body. I didn't know it then but I was experiencing the notion of 'power with'[21] and the sense of the group being greater than the sum of the individuals.

As the afternoon faded into early evening, the students began to disperse, and we made our way back to the bus terminus to board our bus home.

As I stepped down from the bus, I was still caught in the excited conversation with my fellow protestors, our voices temporarily interrupting the quiet of our village before we each went our separate ways. Bernadette and I walked the familiar route home. Snajjin Street, a typical Maltese street, where the doors meet the pavements and each house is decorated to reflect the individuality of its inhabitants. It was exactly the same as it was when I left that morning and yet, I was different. I felt powerful and truly alive in a way I hadn't experienced before. It was as if something had lit up in me, opening my eyes to new possibilities and new perspectives. We walked down the middle of the road as was our custom but today we felt like we owned the place. It was an amazing feeling.

We arrived at Bernadette's house first and said our goodbyes. I continued up the hill to the apartment I lived in. I was so lost in the events of the day that I had no sense of what was about to happen, although thinking about it now I probably did but it was masked by the elation and the excitement I was feeling. I put my key in the lock to open the door, the noise of which must have alerted my father: he was standing there waiting for me. He greeted me with the words, "What the bloody hell do you think you were doing?" which was just the opener to a tirade of angry accusations, much of which I didn't hear as they merged together in my stunned mind. I did hear him tell me several times how irresponsible I was in taking this action; how stupid I was and how disappointed he was in me. He laboured the point that I hadn't given any thought to the impact my actions might have on our residency status on the island.

I stood still and took the full vent of his anger. As his words crushed me, my voice was silenced. I was physically there but emotionally I disconnected from what was happening. I had gone inside myself, escaping his wrath the only way I knew how; by disappearing into my own mind. When he was done with me, I retreated to my room, which was my sanctuary, a place where I could lose myself, where I could feel safe and regain my dignity after such a crushing rebuke. I curled up on my bed and comforted myself with my pillow.

My father never spoke of this event again. Even when the government notice came to say I had been suspended from school for a week, the note was left for me to see but there was no conversation. I shrunk back into my old, familiar shape, fading into the background of our everyday lives, invisible to my parents as they went about their days. It was a well-honed strategy, something I'd learnt to do from a very early age and had repeated so often that it became natural and effortless.

Shortly after the student strike, the government abandoned plans to change the summer holidays and the three-month break remained. Just a couple of years later the female students took a stand again for the right to wear trousers as part of our school uniform. We won that too and because of our action, to this day all female students are allowed to wear trousers.

The whole episode of the strike remained unspoken in our house. As I look back on that day in June, and despite the discomfort of my father's outburst, I'd caught a glimpse of what it felt like to find my voice, to courageously step into my power and to take a stand. That courage came, in part, from being connected to what was important to me while also being connected to my school friends, lifting each other up as we together stepped into the unknown.

Finding voice

I look back on my experience with a renewed appreciation of what it took for us to walk out of school that day. We each connected with something within ourselves that enabled us to show up as more than who we were. For me this meant overcoming my deep-seated fear and anxiety. From my earliest memories I remember feeling afraid. And I was afraid to speak up even when I knew what I wanted to say and felt I could contribute.

Growing up in my family system, speaking up or having my voice heard did not feel safe, let alone valued. I learnt to adapt by getting out of the way, disappearing or keeping myself small. I became hyper-vigilant, paying attention to those around me, tuning into the slightest change, be that in their stance, their mood or their actions, so that I could be ready to respond at any given moment in a way that kept me safe. I learnt to focus on others' needs, rather than my own in order to feel some semblance of belonging. Like any child I yearned to belong, but instead I felt in the way and not wanted. My parents, as a result of their own history rather than any bad intent, were frequently unresponsive to my needs, actively encouraging me to get on with my own life and not bother them. From a very young age I learned not to ask for anything: I became self-reliant, striking out on my own, trying to work things out for myself, not always with the best results.

My family life was in stark contrast to that of my friend, Bernadette. She was one of seven children and as they each arrived home from school, they would gather together around the large kitchen table for tea and home-made cake, talking about their day before settling down to do homework. I remember being surprised by how the older children helped the younger ones with their homework. Education was valued in Bernadette's household but in mine education wasn't given the same prominence. Both my parents had left school at 14 to enter the workplace. Work and working hard was valued and education was simply a necessity, what the law required. I spent many a happy hour in Bernadette's home sitting at their kitchen table. I came to appreciate the value of education and what opens up in the conversations and the sharing of different ideas. I watched how Bernadette's family talked together, laughed together, worked through difficulties together and sometimes even argued with each other. They invited me into their family space and helped me to develop a different interpretation of family; one that I valued and tried to emulate when I became a parent myself. Being with Bernadette's family showed me how there were different ways of being in the world.

We are all products of our history. Our early experiences of family or our primary care givers shape us, but there are other forces at play that influence who we become; the community and the institutions we are part of or the social forces and historical traditions that underpin our society and culture all influence our way of being in the world. Growing up on the island of Malta, I very quickly realised that as a female I was seen as a second-class citizen. I attended an all-girl school at which, as I've shared, we were told that as girls our purpose in life was to get married, to have babies and maintain the family home. In our first year we learnt how to wash a door, clean the cutlery and make our own clothes, all in preparation for married life. In our final year at school, our career advice consisted of a visit to the Phoenicia Hotel in Valletta where we were shown a traditional set of roles: chamber-maid, receptionist or secretary. The notion of gender equality was just that – an idea. The lived reality was male privilege.

Alongside school, religion was also instrumental in keeping many women small, maybe in some cases even more so than family influence. The church played a very strong role in shaping the social structure and mindset of the people on the island. Not only was the cultural expectation that women would marry and have children, and lots of them, women were constantly told that to think about themselves was selfish. We were taught to always put others first and when we married to obey our husbands and never question anything our husbands did. Many women were forced to give up their jobs once they had children because they were no longer allowed to work. Yes, that did happen. As women, our voices were neither encouraged nor wanted.

We exist in these social structures that have their own set of norms and values and they influence our way of being without us even noticing. We've been taught to accept this as normal, for example, the impact of patriarchy and the invisible forces at play that create a system in which women should be small. Just as we're shaped by the families and communities we grew up in, we also shape ourselves in response to our environment. In fact, social context is one of the most influential forces in developing our social and emotional ways of being.

As I entered womanhood and the world of work, I felt powerless to push back against the institutions and established norms I was living inside of. I did what many of my contemporaries did. I got married and then had children. I wanted to be a stay-at-home mum, but as a young family our financial circumstances were such that I needed to work. I knew that if I was going to go back into the workplace, I wanted to be doing something that my boys would be proud of. So alongside working part-time, I embarked on a post-graduate programme of study. Juggling the demands of work with being a young mum while also studying was difficult; I felt I was always running to catch up, never quite feeling on top of anything. Like many of my friends who were also working mums, I felt inadequate, guilty and riddled with self-doubt. The spectre of discrimination was ever present; being told not to apply for a regional role as "you have children", or discovering that my salary fell way short of that of my male colleagues on the management team for no apparent reason. Being told not to rock the boat when I spoke out about my boss's bullish behaviour towards myself and the other women in our team but rather to accommodate it. Or following a business trip to the US, I boarded my transatlantic flight home only to discover that the seat I'd been given was broken and watching as a male passenger was upgraded and I was moved into his seat! I was shocked and yet paralysed, unable to do anything other than comply. When I did raise it with the airline, I was told, "let me assure you, Madam, we do not discriminate, I will send you some air miles!" Realising that my dignity was worth so little was a huge wake-up call. I've lost count of the times I arrived for a management meeting and was asked to take notes as, and I'm sure many of you reading this will have heard: "because you have nice writing!" While they may be harmless in their intent, these norms of behaviour serve to keep us stuck in a pattern unable to see just what really is being produced.

Inside of this social context my embodied shape brought me strength too. I was well practised at being hyper-vigilant, scanning for safety, adjusting to belong and so I paid attention to building the relationship, creating a space with those I interacted with that fostered trust and connection. I'd also learnt to keep myself small in my family system and it was second nature to do exactly the same in the workplace, deferring to my male colleagues just as I deferred to my father. I worked hard, responding to what was needed, often exceeding what was asked of me. I avoided any visibility, actively side-stepping having the attention on me or anything I'd achieved which was often in contrast to male colleagues who seemed adept at making their achievements public and often won by being singularly focused on the task at hand, privileging logic and reason over emotions all in pursuit of the goal. Whereas I valued relationships, the human connection, and getting things done with people. High-profile businesswoman Mary Portas[22] suggests that, "… most businesses have an alpha working culture. And it's a culture that respects and rewards so called 'masculine' qualities, like risk-taking, competition and single minded, myopic focus… the drive to 'win'". The qualities of empathy, intuition and trust were seen as unimportant and at odds with the prevailing culture.

I believed the way to navigate this system more effectively was to seek more knowledge: if I learnt more, gained a higher qualification or two, then somehow it would be the key to unlock those opportunities that had alluded me thus far. And so I embarked first on a post-graduate qualification, then a master's followed by a doctorate. However, seeking more knowledge only took me so far. Why? Because I embodied a way of being that was immune to my intellect and my brain. I couldn't just tell myself to show up differently, to be more confident or more assertive. In those moments when I found myself under pressure, or in a new and challenging situation, I would still shrink away, unable to speak my truth, surrendering any power or influence I might have had. I felt a hostage to my own shape, caught in my conditioned responses, navigating whatever life threw at me the only way I knew how, on automatic pilot. I could not think my way to be different and so I felt powerless to challenge the workplace culture.

Then something happened that opened my eyes to the possibility that things could be different. Greg Dyke arrived at the BBC as the new director general and launched 'One BBC', with the aim of making the Corporation 'the most creative organisation in the world', creating a flatter structure, breaking down silos and promoting greater collaboration. 'Making it Happen' was born. It was both bold and ambitious for its time, a culture change programme which challenged existing organisational paradigms and more than once broke new ground. I was thrilled to be part of the internal consulting team working on this. At its core, the change Making it Happen was seeking to make was alive in the method used and in those of us working with it. The relational methodology we adopted privileged the building of personal relationships, engaging the whole community. Indeed, 'Just Imagine', the discovery phase of Making it Happen, was one of the world's largest Appreciative Inquiries[23], in which 10,000 BBC staff participated in workshops redesigning the organisation's culture, workplaces, audience relationships and people policies. I was struck by the power of conversation, the honouring of people in the system, the recognition of their humanity and the importance placed on everyone being given a voice in shifting the system. It was organisation development thought leader Roger Harrison[24] who suggested that inviting individuals and groups to speak their truth was key to transformation and at the BBC we were doing just that.

The whole experience of Making it Happen had woken me up; I was rubbing my eyes and beginning to see differently, that I could be different, that the workplace could be different and I was hungry for more. I was finding my voice and the courage to speak my truth.

Moving beyond

In her inspirational speech at the 2018 Golden Globe Awards, Oprah Winfrey said, "What I know for sure is that speaking your truth is the most powerful tool we all have." I had a conversation with one of my clients, Anja Wideburg, who at the time was vice president talent & leadership at Yara International, and she told me, "we are all individuals and the one thing I can give is my own truth. I can influence because my truth is what people want to follow." And yet, for many women leaders, speaking their truth is hard, not least because their identity, and potentially their career, is at stake. It calls for courage to go against societal norms and power.

We have to find our own internal power in order to move into courage. Yet the very word power conjures up problems. Anja explained it to me this way: in German the word power can be translated as either *macht* or *kraft*, each with its own definition: the word *macht* is typically used when referring to positional power where one person uses or abuses their power to dominate another, leaving them with little or no choice. We only have to think about the suffragette movement and the women who fought bravely to have the right to vote. They came up against the positional power, or *macht*, of the political institutions and society at large that sought to maintain the status quo.

On the other hand, *kraft* has a very different kind of energy; it's a power that comes from within, knowing self-worth, able to be vulnerable, honest and transparent. For Anja this means living in the question, 'how can I be in peace with myself and with others?' What Anja points us to is how when we speak our truth, and we allow ourselves to be seen, society or others around us may push back. This is when we need to be even more courageous and stand our ground, digging deep and truly listening to ourselves, allowing our truth to emerge.

Working on the 'Making it Happen' programme at the BBC led to an 'a-ha' moment for me. I experienced the possibilities that are created when relationships, community and voice are honoured at the centre of what we do. And when I truly listened to myself, I felt this pull towards creating spaces where people in organisations could engage in deep meaningful conversations with each other. I didn't want to settle for an alpha working culture, I wanted to work towards restoring humanity in the workplace. My offer would be far-reaching, in that it would profoundly touch how people felt. It would reconnect them with what they care about. I couldn't articulate what that might look like, even less be able to speak to it; all I knew was that this nebulous need had been stirred in me. I felt courageous and, seeing an opportunity to make a bigger contribution, I decided to leave my corporate life and set up my own consultancy. I was stepping into the unknown. As an unlikely entrepreneur I was full of self-doubt and afraid about the future but wanted to embrace it all as I felt it would drive me forward. I knew deep down that this was the right move for me to make.

With very little work in the pipeline, I embarked on this new phase in my life by getting on a plane to Nova Scotia, Canada, to attend the Shambhala Authentic Leadership Programme. Founded by the late Michael Chander, this annual event was an amazing gathering of leaders and practitioners from across the world. That first day at the conference, I found myself sitting round a table with a group of seriously experienced leaders. The inevitable moment arrived when we each had to introduce ourselves. What was I going to say? For the last ten years I'd introduced myself by saying that I worked for the BBC and people immediately became interested, eager to hear more. Someone somewhere has seen *Doctor Who, Top Gear, Walking with Dinosaurs* or even *Strictly Come Dancing* (*Dancing with the Stars* as it is known outside the UK). There was the inevitable question about a celebrity, often followed by a genuine interest in just what it was like to be on the inside, with a playful curiosity about what was going to happen in the next episode of *Sherlock*. So being able to say, "I work for the BBC" had been a wonderful diversion from any questions about me. In that moment, I realised just how much my professional identity had been wrapped up in those three letters. I could feel the familiar feeling of wanting to disappear and make myself small, not helped by the person introducing herself before me stating that she was an astronaut who worked for NASA and had been into space twice on the space shuttle. How was I to follow that?! I took a deep breath and launched in. Despite my somewhat clunky introduction, the response was very different to what I had expected; people were genuinely interested, interrupting my automatic internal narrative.

During the week I found myself in very different conversations to those I'd been used to. We explored how we were each showing up in our practice and what we were each drawn to in our work. Throughout the week, I had the privilege to meet and learn from a number of thought leaders in the field, each workshop inviting me into new perspectives and challenging me to go beyond my self imposed limitations. I attended a workshop led by embodiment teacher Arawana Hayashi. In the first session I experienced for the first time the power of learning with the body. Arawana invited the group to be in the present moment, to tune into a deeper part of ourselves, a part of us that lives underneath the façade of role, job title and any of the projections we may take on from others. Through a series of human moves, lying, sitting and standing, my awareness opened, and I came face to face with my habitual way of being in the world – an all-too-familiar pattern of striving to get the movement 'right', which of course meant checking to see if I was where everyone else was in the sequence rather than recognising that there was nowhere to be but where I was! A well-honed strategy that belied the fear I felt. And yet I felt curiously drawn-in. There was something in Arawana's own way of being that captured my attention. I watched as this petite, quietly spoken woman exuded a confidence, an authority, a gravitas, that seemed to emanate from a place of deeper understanding that went beyond cognitive knowing to an embodiment of all she is, a way of being that was compelling.

Our hosts for that week-long conference, Marianne Knuth, Tim Merry and Sera Thompson operated from a truly authentic connection with themselves and who they are. It was as if there was an invisible connection between them and the ground underneath them. They were not just talking at us or directing the conversation in a pre-ordained way, rather they each entered the flow of the discourse, blending with what was emerging in the moment, provoking and challenging when appropriate while getting out of the way too. I could feel how they were deeply invested in what was being created in the space, they brought as much of themselves as they asked us to.

My time at Shambhala was another wake-up call. I felt as if I'd been shaken from a 100-year sleep where my 'feeling self' had been frozen in time, and I began to hear a new voice emerging from somewhere deep within me 'that I slowly recognised as my own' as the poet Mary Oliver[25] says. That week in Nova Scotia had given me a taste of what was possible. It left me feeling somewhat unsettled and yet compelled to continue on this path. There was no turning back.

I engaged in a programme of deep inner work. Through skilful coaching I was able to shift those deeply held habitual patterns that shaped my very being, take off the layers of shame and heal the trauma that lived in my body. I learnt how to centre and get present, transcending my mood of fear that kept me small, to a mood of courage, which allowed me to see possibilities for myself. By turning my attention inwards, I was able to tune into the here-and-now sensations that are ever present in our physical structure: those of heat or cold, pressure or openness, aliveness or numbness. I became aware of how I armour myself, where in my body I habitually contract and how I habitually disconnect from myself. I learnt how to access safety for myself rather than defaulting to my historical conditioning, dwelling more deeply inside myself. I was encouraged to create new practices that supported me and allowed me to take care of my own needs for the first time in my life.

As I practised turning my attention inward, I became increasingly connected with what's important to me. I began to align my actions with what I care about, moving beyond my fear to show up authentically. As I became more able and accustomed to speaking my truth, I was surprised to see that people not only wanted to listen but they wanted to engage with me too.

By being in my own work (and continually challenging myself) I've stepped into opportunities I could only have dreamed of as that young 12-year-old girl walking down Republic Street in Malta. I have more choice in how I act and respond. I've developed a new relationship with power, one that comes from within, and stepped into the truth of who I am – the kind of power Anja would describe as *kraft*. By literally shifting my shape, moving from being contained and narrow to being more expansive and open, I'm able to be a bigger contribution, generating new possibilities for my clients. It still takes great courage for me to find my voice and be heard, to stand tall and be truly present but now I can centre inside of what's important to me, what I care about, feel my ground underneath me and step into my power.

The success of the leadership and organisation development consultancy I founded has seen me work with a network of coaches and consultants among the best in the field. I have been coaching leaders, executive teams and organisations, building their capacity to navigate the space of emergence by accessing their personal power. More recently, I've been working with a range of organisations to shift their leadership culture and female representation at senior levels by enabling women leaders to find their purpose, voice and authentic authority for maximum impact at work. Women develop their own interpretation of power, one that moves away from the traditional 'power over', or *macht*, to a sense and interpretation of power that enables them to make things happen. They report feeling more confident in handling conflict, more comfortable with uncertainty, more resilient in the midst of challenging demands and more inclined to speak their truth. By learning to self-regulate in the moment, the women we work with no longer feel hostage to their historical conditioning but are able to show up more powerfully and more effectively as female leaders in the workplace, often becoming more than they thought they could be.

As women, we're conditioned to seek outside of ourselves for help, to look for rules and corporate structures and systems (all of which have their place, as I've previously mentioned) to fix the issue. But my purpose, and that of my work and this book, is to show that we have the capacity and the power for change within us. And I believe we have a responsibility as women to shift how we're showing up. For once we shift, everything around us shifts in some way too – it cannot stay the same (this is the power of the #MeToo movement).

Shifting our historical and social conditioning that shapes what it means to be a woman in today's world is hard; our stories, our history, the social forces which shape our world-view become familiar and comfortable. It's a journey, an adventure even, that has a mixture of surprises, drama and excitement. Along the way we discover new ways to make sense of what's unfolding for us. By doing our own work and reclaiming ourselves as women, we can learn to show up with a strong presence, one that embodies confidence, cultivates trust and psychological safety, enables greater ease and builds authentic connection. When as women we begin to practise new ways of being in our interactions, we become an invitation to others to respond in new and different ways. It's the interconnectedness between individual and collective transformation that begins to shift the culture and opens the possibility for a more inclusive workplace. As Håkan Petersson (who at the time of working with him was the Head of L&D North and East Europe for E.ON) observed, "I have seen a number of our women leaders realising their potential and successfully moving into executive board level roles. They not only embody the capacity to meet the changing needs of the business but have a wider influence on our leadership culture." Inclusiveness is now a business imperative; forward-thinking organisations know the value of an inclusive workplace and senior level female representation is great for the bottom line.

Please be clear though – I'm not talking about changing to fit into a male-dominated space, 'leaning in', being 'one of the boys' or being 'fixed' because in some way we're at fault. Instead, it's about reclaiming ourselves as women in a way that makes us no longer accountable to our own histories or the systems created in our society. It's about doing the work which frees us to be truly and authentically ourselves, cultivating our identity as women, and stepping into our power. And if we can do this collectively, by coming together, supporting one another and having each others' backs, we can begin to break down the norms and social forces to create spaces where everyone, women *and* men, can show up authentically, treating each other as human beings.

In a recent article published in *Forbes* Shelly Zalis, CEO, The Female Quotient, writes, "a woman alone has power; collectively we have impact" and calls for us to raise each other up and channel the power of collaboration.[26]

In the spirit of raising each other up, five courageous women have stepped forward to share their stories. As Michelle Obama tells us, "Your story is what you have, what you will always have. It is something to own."[27] In the following chapters you'll hear from some of these women as they share their stories; how they were shaped by their histories and how through their own personal struggles they rose above numerous limitations and expectations placed on them by others. You'll hear how they've come to know themselves in a deeply human way – a way that gives them more choice, more control and more power. Power of the *kraft* kind, through which they can lead and serve others genuinely, and with humility.

Before you turn the page, you may like to reflect on this question:

What is being provoked in you now when you think about your own relationship with power?

An invitation to practice – Tuning in

As you think about this question, what's being provoked in you about your own relationship with power. Rather than answering it from your head, I'd like to invite you to simply sit with that question and notice what comes up. Our western society privileges our intellectual, rational, intelligence and I'm certainly not arguing against that, but we have a huge supply of unused intelligence that resides below the neck. We begin to access this powerful, and dare I say ancient, wisdom by becoming more aware and more conscious of how we are being in the moment. We do this by bringing our attention to our physical sensations. For example, sensations of warmth or coolness, pressure or tension, movement or numbness. By simply being aware of our bodily sensations we can begin to wake up to the wisdom of the body.

Try this for yourself:

Just for a moment, turn your attention inwards and as you do so, notice the various physical sensations present in your body: are your shoulders tense or your teeth clenched; is your breath high and shallow, are you holding your diaphragm, perhaps creating a knot in your stomach?

As you become conscious of your shape ask yourself what occurred for you as you tuned into your own sensations? As you explore this territory, invite more relaxation by letting your shoulders relax, dropping your breath to the abdomen and softening your jaw.

Bringing our attention to the life of the body, and its wisdom, and shifting our shape in the moment, allows us to be more present to ourselves and responsive to what is happening internally and externally.

As you go back to that question, what emerges for you now?

Let me now introduce you to Fernanda Lopes Larsen who is the SVP for indirect procurement at Yara International, an organisation dedicated to responsibly feeding the world and protecting the planet. I first met Fernanda as a participant in the Yara Women's Executive Programme, a programme we co-designed to enable women to become more powerful and authentic female leaders. I continued to work with Fernanda beyond the programme as her coach. I'm inspired by Fernanda's unwavering commitment to developing herself as a leader so that she might empower more women leaders to find their voice. Fernanda is making a significant contribution in enabling Scandinavian women of colour to navigate the challenges of the corporate world. In her own organisation, she has influenced a renewed focus on diversity and inclusion and is now leading a programme of work.

In her chapter, Fernanda awakens us to how we come to embody the social conditions we grow up and live in. She illustrates how women continue to find themselves living and working in systems of power in which access to fundamental human needs of safety, belonging and dignity are denied. And she tells how, instead of running away from her past and who she is, she learned to use her life experience to embody a new and more powerful leadership; one that calls out the voices of prejudice, one that values her voice and encourages her to honour her own history.

Chapter Two

Belonging

Fernanda Lopes Larsen
The game of my life

As I waited for others to arrive into the elegantly furnished executive meeting room on the sixth floor, I couldn't help but feel reinvigorated by the sunny and beautiful view of the city's skyline. Taking the opportunity to reflect on the extraordinary journey I'd been part of up to that moment – a journey of professional and personal growth, with all the ups and downs it entails – filled my body with a sudden burst of energy and a renewed sense of passion for my job and for my team.

The same passion and energy were also palpable in all other 30 team members or so who'd finally arrived for the ceremony that was about to unveil. Excitement, loud chatting and giggling were filling all corners of the room. People were recounting success stories, challenges, dramas, reliving funny situations and detailing word by word every moment of their contributions towards that historic moment for the department. We, the central procurement organization, had over-delivered on our targets in a year that was one of the toughest in our company's history. And they, the Brazilian team gathered in that room, represented a vital share of procurement's total success. More than in any other region, Brazilian Procurement fought difficult market and economic conditions, scarce internal resources, conflicting priorities and yet managed to deliver improvements that by many were deemed impossible. Leading this team was one of the most transformational experiences of my career, for it taught me how to connect different geographies, cultures and drive organizational change by managing the fine balance between central steering and local needs.

To celebrate our accomplishments in a symbolic way we would throw several plastic balls into a cylinder, each ball representing a million-dollar savings achieved by the organization. The president of the Brazilian division joined us, and his inspiring words echoed across the room making us all feel connected, united, accomplished and full of purpose. I complemented his words by saying that we were the true representation of the power of working as one, the real embodiment of determination and cross-border collaboration.

Finished with our speeches, we then moved to the ball-throwing ceremony. The president had the first go and while doing so managed to land the first ball from a very long distance straight into the cylinder. We all laughed, applauded and congratulated him on his 'NBA worthy' abilities. We joked that basketball would have been an excellent career choice for him as well, to which he laughed and concurred. Then it was my turn.

As a global senior vice president of procurement in the company, a lot of that success we were celebrating had to do with my organization and how my team navigated resistance, volatility and change with skill and determination. I felt an enormous sense of pride but also responsibility as I held the plastic ball in my hands. And once again that so familiar feeling of *"cannot fail, this is my only shot"* was present. As I threw the ball, it stubbornly kicked from one side to the other of the cylinder, bouncing on its edge, changing its course from left to right, refusing to enter the recipient, but also refusing to succumb to the floor... In that exact moment, while all in the room cheered in suspense waiting to see what would happen next, I then realized: *that plastic ball symbolized the story of my life.*

(Un)fair play

I grew up in a small town in the countryside of Brazil. Daughter of a working-class family, there was, simply put, nothing extraordinary about my childhood and adolescence. A stay-at-home mother, an older brother and a father who worked hard to provide us with food, clothes and special private schooling in a country where public education was not necessarily associated with quality. I went to a Salesian Catholic school, had lots of friends, enjoyed summer holidays on the coast and had middle-class life plans for the future like everybody else.

My family and I are black. And while the importance of this fact wasn't fully clear to me as a child, it grew in significance as I became older and started to understand the societies around me, and their unwritten rules. My non-belonging into a white society not only became gradually visible through the curious and seemingly innocent comments about my hair, but also grew in harshness and intensity as I turned into a young woman.

The de-humanizing insinuations that 'bananas should be my favorite fruit' became replaced by the loneliness of not having a boyfriend in my teens, by the absence of a black friend figure who could relate to my adolescence experiences and most of all, by the inexistence of types like me in any of the social circles I was part of. I quickly realized that something about my world was indeed very 'off' and the realities of life were finally hitting me. The bricks of the protection walls my parents so wholeheartedly and lovingly put around me and my brother were starting to ruin, for we grew up in a white world that seemed not to want to grant us the same rights and advantages like everyone else.

The awareness of gender inequalities started to become visible around the same time. Being a black girl seemed most of the time significantly harder than being a black boy. My brother's active and vibrant social life, fuelled by his popularity and extrovert ways, seemed to act as a perfect cover for his 'blackness', casting at the same time a shadow on my own teenage life. Constantly compared with him, I quickly gained the reputation of unsympathetic, closed-up and 'not like my brother.' Many times, I was referred to only as my brother's sister, nameless, without my proper identity or right to exist on my own account. The Latin Catholic culture acted as a catalyst to these inequalities, giving boys the priority of rank, while relegating girls like me to a secondary role of invisibility. I vividly recall my confusion at times trying to reconcile the disparity between Christian teachings of fairness and justice and the rules of the game I was daily subjected to. How could the world be fair if I was the only one supposed to help with housework? Why could I only get my driving license after my brother? Why should women remain in unhappy marriages just because the church expects them to (this one almost cost me an expulsion from my confirmation classes)?

To be perfectly honest, the manifestations of gender imbalance in my family were mostly mild in nature and relatively harmless in consequences. Despite the occasional adolescent frustrations, I enjoyed a lot of freedom and positive empowerment from my parents and close relatives and was encouraged to follow my path of choice from a very early age. Female empowerment, in particular, took a rather peculiar shape in my household. The women in my life – mainly my mother and my *tias* (the Portuguese word for aunts) – were an essential part of my growing up and filled my life not only with colors, warmth and delicious food, but also with powerful advice, that on one side seemed extremely conflicting but, when analysed under the lens of the time carried enormous wisdom, power and progressiveness. This way, it wasn't unusual for me to be constantly reminded by them of my duty to help with household chores because "that is a woman's job", and at the same time be given long sermons of how essential education was to avoid me ending up 'like them'.

These women in my life – the frustrated mother, the unhappily married or the single and childless aunts – were the first female role models of my life. They would all portray themselves as examples of what not to become, but unbeknownst to them, they were my real sources of strength and adoration, for I learned from them the value of hard work, courage, and honesty. Succeeding in life became my way to repay them for their sacrifices and unconditional love. And I definitely took the task to heart.

Creating my own rules

I realized early enough that I was smart and that the combination of intellect, determination and grit was a powerful formula for success. Granted with the status of 'brainy' provided me with a passport for protection and acceptance. Being a stellar student became my weapon to break barriers and enter rooms where I wasn't openly welcome. I embraced the mindset that only through sheer intellectual force and discipline would I be able to conquer my place in the world. When opportunities presented themselves, I embraced them wholeheartedly because, simply put, there might not be a second one.

Genetics was also on my side. I inherited my father's abilities with numbers and managed to blaze through high school with straight A grades in physics, math and chemistry. Therefore, my decision to pursue engineering didn't come as a surprise to anyone in the family, and in 1992 I joined one of the country's elite universities, following a laborious 12 months of dedicated studies to clear the admission tests. Once at university, I continued pursuing my philosophy of non-deviation and lived through my academic years with herculean determination and focus, aiming to be, once more, the number one student. It was, after all, a proven formula whose ingredients I wasn't willing to risk changing. This recipe was my survival strategy.

Honestly speaking, I cannot recall having any fun during my university years in Brazil. However, I do recall the yet again familiar face of discrimination and racism, which this time presented itself in even more cruel ways. Internships or job interviews with no answer, harassment by cliques of girls, malicious comments about my appearance, all brought up memories of a system I was so very determined to fight. And as my academic years went on, my social and racial awareness reached peak levels. The more injustice I saw, the more I started to openly question the world around me, challenging notions, questioning rules and claiming my place in the world. I did dare to dream, to demand, and to refuse what wasn't good enough in my view.

I was determined to travel roads that my family and their ancestors never thought possible to travel.

One of these roads led me eventually to Europe. Being the first generation in my family to have a university degree, I also became the first generation to have an international degree. Granted with a scholarship from the Austrian government to pursue my master's in Civil Engineering, I later joined the European corporate world, working for a large American multinational in Germany.

Europe was at the beginning a true breath of fresh air from the cruel racial and social realities of Brazil. The openness, the debate, the social equality, all made me feel like I belonged, much more than I'd ever felt in my home country. For some time, I even resisted participating in corporate diversity initiatives because there seemed to be no real issue to address. I was in my early twenties, doing really well in my job, fully integrated into German society and for once, the happiest I'd ever been in my entire life. So, when my boss at the time suggested I join the company's affinity group for black female employees, I politely declined. I could not see any need for it. The system was perfectly fair in my view. He was surprised at my reaction but patiently and wisely replied: "you are not seeing the need now, but as you progress in your career, it will become very visible to you."

I never forgot his words, because it didn't take long for me to realize how right he'd been.

Lost in translation

The thing with prejudice and discrimination is, their effects never truly leave you. As a stamp, they print marks in one's soul that are hard to erase. They fill one with doubts, destroy self-confidence and erect walls that impede one from opening up and accepting new possibilities in their lives. And so, as I moved up the career ladder, the scars of prejudice and injustice started to tingle again. I was exposed to corporate politics, being passed up for promotions, not getting the visibility and opportunities I felt I deserved. And my reaction to all this was to become even more combative, mistrustful, closed up, sabotaging myself, and my chances even more. I moved companies, countries (left Germany for the UK), business areas, and yet I was struggling to find voice and meaning. Some mid-management opportunities still presented themselves to me, but it soon became clear that my proven formula of discipline, grit and resilience wasn't doing the trick anymore. Leadership was a much more complex road that demanded something deeper and more sophisticated from me. Poise, ability to influence, to inspire, to compromise and accept defeat with grace were all new ingredients to me.

I was struggling to express myself, to find my ground and my balance. I was either being brutally (and non-politically correct) honest or not bringing my voice at all, shutting myself down in frustration, painting enemies where there were none and feeding my anger whenever complex challenges presented themselves in my way. I also had enormous difficulties in saying no; after all, my life's mantra was built on the belief that opportunities present themselves only once, and if I, as a black woman, get thrown out of course once, I would pay the price eternally.

The height of these internal struggles happened when I moved to Norway. Under severe cultural shock and still grieving my departure from the UK, navigating the Norwegian corporate world was a baptism of fire. Built on a culture of consensus and avoidance of conflicts, Norwegians tend to be reserved individuals who take immense pride in resolving issues through several rounds of discussions and alignments. This in my world translated as torture. Suddenly I felt that being myself was totally wrong, after all I was an extroverted, opinionated and extremely driven woman, exuding energy to get things resolved as quickly as possible.

I became more and more frustrated with the status quo, with the difficulties of getting the vision I had for my area to prevail, of relating to stakeholders who had a completely opposite way of behaving. And so, I made a personal resolution to leave my current job and apply for an internal position in the US, thinking that changing country again, rather than changing my reaction to situations, was the best alternative.

So, as I prepared for the conversation with my manager, I knew deep down that giving up was exactly not what I wanted to do.

The power of an opportunity

It was a very simple but long conversation. I explained how I felt like a "fish out of the pond" in my current job, different and disconnected from everyone and everything. While my peers seemed so knowledgeable and 100% involved in the company's day-to-day operations, I was convinced I couldn't keep up with their experiences or speak their language. And I was not being able to reconcile my expertise in the strategic procurement field with the ways of working of our company in Europe, for I believed vision and strategy were important steps that kept being relegated to second plan vis-à-vis the daily operational needs.

I'd also arrogantly concluded that culture difference was the one plausible explanation. And like in a failing love relationship the best alternative for me was to stoically part ways and move on to the familiar Anglo-Saxon environment, which in my mind would magically resolve everything. A new job. A familiar culture. An escape…

She listened attentively, like she always did in every of our conversations, nodding her head and looking fiercely into my eyes, absorbing every word in a respectful silence. Then in her calm voice she asked: "And why do you think that your peers are right, and you are wrong? How do you know that you are not having a positive impact by 'being different.'"

Those words hit me like thunder. And in my astonishment, I simply had no answer for her, because it had never crossed my mind until that point that the problems I was facing were not the result of cultural differences, but rather the perks of leadership, and overcoming those, instead of escaping them, was in fact the key part of my job. My task was to navigate that operational maze while instilling a sense of strategic direction for the procurement function. It was to transform, to bring poise and focus to the heated everyday discussions with my peers and stakeholders. It was to support and guide my team as they were confronted with similar difficulties daily. And step-by-step, I would help plant the seeds that would grow into a better culture and more understanding between the areas. Every time I questioned standard practices, I was unconsciously doing that. Every time I took the time to explain things from my point of view, I went a step further into contributing to change and transformation. Every time I listened, I grew as a leader.

Further reflecting at night and still flustered from that conversation, I started to comprehend even more how amazing the opportunity I was being presented with was. A supportive female manager who showed full trust in my potential and presented herself open and willing to let me learn, discover, fail and grow. For the first time in my career I was being given a chance to experiment with senior leadership in its entirety, yet under the wings of protection and wisdom of a leader who inspired me to achieve more and never give up. A leader who didn't see color, differences but only potential. A leader who showed to me the power of the first chance. The power of incentive. The power of trust.

And so, a feeling of determination filled my heart and I decided I was going to stay and embrace the experience fully. Free from political agendas and moved by the ambition to have my team succeed, we delivered the business case of a very complex project, propelling my area and myself to even higher heights.

I was then promoted to senior vice president of procurement. The first black woman to do so in my company. Probably in

Scandinavia. And once again managed by the same supportive leader, who kept displaying full trust in my abilities and potential.

Learning to learn again

However, as I onboarded into my new senior role, I was confronted by difficulties. Seen as a 'protégé' of my boss, as the 'diversity woman' who only managed the procurement top position because of my gender and color, once again sexism and prejudice were plaguing my life. The sudden weight of being exposed and put on an 'altar' of role-modelling for other ethnic and female employees also became at one point too much to bear. The initial satisfaction of the dozens of supportive emails received upon the event of my promotion was quickly replaced by a full-blown imposter syndrome. And so, more than ever before I felt I could simply not fail. More than ever before I couldn't disappoint my boss and all the trust she'd put on me. I was determined to succeed to prove them wrong, but my energy was not matching my ambition and determination, for everything around me made me believe that I didn't deserve to be in that place.

Around the same time, as if by a divine (or maybe my boss's?) intervention, I was invited to join a women's executive program, the first of its kind in the company. Reluctant at first and afraid to be typecast forever as a diversity token, I still decided to embrace this opportunity, which became the most important turning point in my career. Surrounded by other senior female leaders and in the comfort of a safe and open environment, we talked, we opened up, we connected. And suddenly those feelings of loneliness and solitude started to vanish. Female colleagues from all over the world experienced similar dilemmas, faced exactly the same circumstances and doubts as I did.

During the program we came into close contact with the principles of somatics. Learning how to pay attention to the signs of my body was a life-changing revelation, for it enabled me to be aware of the quality of my presence and how others perceived me. My energy, according to the trainers, was solely concentrated on my upper body and to improve my presence, I had to re-distribute it. Breathing, centering, feeling my body in the space. Alone. Or fully synchronized with my female peers, jo kata in my hands, the power and the calm that came with every movement was an exhilaration of emotions and release. Release of what I truly am. And of what I wanted to be.

Having decided to explore further what had been opened in that women's program, I engaged in one-to-one bi-weekly lessons with one of the facilitators, not sure exactly about what the outcome would be, but fully open to discover it. And every session was an epiphany. Different from a standard coaching session, my coach's questions would lead me to powerful inner discoveries that would shake me to the core. How to navigate my moods and frustrations, how to turn negatives into positives and how to understand my circle of influence became not only 'coaching lessons' but rather powerful medicine that opened up a plethora of ways to manage my energy and anxieties in a better way. I was finally on a path to discover what actually worked for me.

The high point of this discovery journey was the declaration of my purpose. Until that point, success in my view was a vertical line, represented only by promotions and ascension. But as I recited my purpose out loud several times, the 'little black Brazilian girl' started to give space to the mature black leader that didn't have to prove anything to anyone anymore. My purpose of "bringing depth and openness in the pursuit of fairness and equality" became my true north. Self-fulfillment took a very different form and I started to leverage my senior position and status to benefit others instead.

Helping women in my company became my side job. I mentored and held space for them, sponsored their careers and advocated on their behalf. I also focused on educating male colleagues on the issues and possibilities of corporate diversity. To influence employees and leaders, to elevate the level of the debate around diversity, all I needed to do was to bring my own experiences, my own stories to the table. Stories of hardship and insecurities, but also of immense power, love, values and compassion.

That was my power. It wasn't in my title, or in my position. But simply in who I was and am.

Not always a SLAM DUNK, but still winning

My leadership journey continues being one of self-discovery and continuous learning. I'm clear now that not only the destination is less important than the journey but the target is constantly moving. I'll always continue evolving, changing and re-setting. And that's perfectly fine. For harnessing the power that comes with opening up oneself to new possibilities is the best part of the adventure. Being open for exquisite experiences and embracing the self-confidence that comes with it is exhilarating. The same self-confidence I displayed by going back to the university and taking up further business studies. The same self-confidence I showed when approaching my CEO on a pledge to help me change corporate diversity in the Nordics.

As I embrace my purpose, I'm strategizing and finding new ways to be fulfilled and re-energized. I'm exercising the power of gratitude to fight the curses of frustration. I'm focusing on fostering relationships that enable me to share my full and unexcused female black experience, matching my energy with the environments I'm part of, while staying true to myself. But most importantly, mentoring and helping women find their ways, while sharing my experiences with others is the real thrill which fills me with confidence and hunger for more. It enables me to fight the moments where I do feel I'm not good enough or that I don't deserve to be where I am. It enables me to be a proud black woman, in a white corporate environment, whose mission is to change the game. I want to look back and be the woman who helped others. The women who paved the way for my daughter to achieve even more. The woman whose mother and *tias* taught well.

The fear sometimes is still very present. Palpable. And probably it will always be. There are times when everything simply fits and falls into place nicely. Other times, it's total emotional mayhem. Ups and downs. Back and forth. Out and in. Like the plastic ball I threw that morning. No clear slam dunk. But yet nicely inside the cylinder. Together with the others, where it belonged.

What the research revealed...

Research theme one: The power of re-authoring our interpretation of power, creating a new definition that aligns with our own individual values and vision.

We're products of our history and as women we embody the historical and social forces of what it means to be a woman in the world. What we embody informs how we interpret power, how we act with power and how we construct our identity as female leaders. The women spoke of having inherited an interpretation of power that is 'power over', with many associating the word 'power' with words like dominating, authoritative, controlling and hierarchical. I found that for those women who'd dismantled their inherited interpretation of power and created a new definition that more closely aligned to their own values and vision, a shift in their way of being happened too. By re-authoring the definition they'd inherited, the norms they'd grown up with and continue to live in, they were able to create a new relationship with power.

Deborah Whitworth-Hilton, Gas Storage Operations Manager UK for Uniper, shared with me, "in the past power was an aggressive word for me and conjured up either the image of 'men in suits' or 'aggressive women'. I have learnt that power is an individual thing and I can feel the power from within and achieve great results."

Sandy DeFelice, Pre-sales Director, SAS, told me, "my leadership now emerges in the stillness of owning my power."

In her chapter, 'Cultivating the Still Point: The Power of Reflective Leadership'[28], author and leadership consultant Ellen Wingard suggests that it's in the quiet that we can cultivate the still point which is the place where "our intellect, emotions, instincts, light and shadow converge to reflect our core being."

When a leader is able to shift her historical interpretation of power, she is able to build authentic relationships, create followership and make things happen.

An invitation to reflect
What has shaped me?

Our experiences live in our body. By paying attention to the body, our mood and emotions, our thoughts, we begin to discover what is embodied in us. Fernanda's story invites us all to come to know how our history shapes us. To begin to explore this, I draw on the Sites of Shaping model developed by Alan Grieg and generationFIVE[29]. This framework enables us to see how the different influences in our lives have shaped us and how our different life experiences become embodied habits inside of us. It helps us increase our awareness of how we show up, our default habits and patterns and our values.

What has shaped you? You may like to reflect on these questions:

Individual
- How would you describe your nature, what you were born with?

Family and intimate network
- How have your experiences of family and/or your primary caregivers shaped who you are today? What values did they have?

Community
- What are the different communities you grew up in? How did these communities influence who you are today?

Institution
- Think about the different institutions you've been part of, be that your school or university, being part of the armed forces or working inside of a corporation? Choose one or two and think about how they influence how you act and interact and how you see the world?

Social norms and historical forces
- What have you been taught to accept as 'normal', for example the impact of patriarchy and the social expectations on women?

Spirit and landscape
- How does the physical environment shape you? Are you drawn to a spiritual path, for example, and if so, how does this show up in how you show up?

It's helpful for us to remember that we're always living inside of this complex network of forces. It's the water we're swimming in and it's embodied so we may not notice or question what feels familiar to us. By separating out the different forces in our lives we can begin to deepen our awareness of the history we each embody.

Just imagine… you are an HR director. Your company has been in the headlines for weeks for unethical behaviour. The media is poised outside your front door day and night. This has resulted in the immediate closure of a product and several hundred people are being made redundant. Your chairman and his son have been publicly questioned by a parliamentary committee. Having reviewed the company records given to them, the police have started home raids on your staff.

In her chapter, Carrie Birmingham shares with us the challenges of being that HR director, a senior female leader, navigating a crisis in an alpha male culture. Her story invites us into the question, who do I need to be as a leader in this context? Carrie illustrates the power of presence, how she was able to tune into herself while simultaneously tuning into what was emerging all around her, and find her own ground and hold it, in order to help others find theirs. By expanding her capacity to get present she could then take action from a deeper sense of awareness.

Today, Carrie is the founder of her own business dedicated to supporting leaders and organisations to fix messy and complex problems through coaching and consultancy.

Chapter Three

Warrior spirit

Carrie Birmingham

M y story is about a headstrong and driven woman, a fighter who's been tested to her limits, but has along the way learned to adapt and change, emerging instead as a Warrior Spirit, one who combines strength with tenderness, challenge with connection, with a clear purpose to enable justice wherever possible. This journey has involved accepting some uncomfortable truths about myself along with some hugely difficult experiences but it's allowed me to understand who I truly am, be choiceful about how I work with others and to thoughtfully consider ways in which I might find my power to make a difference.

For me this spirit is captured in the *Fearless Girl* statue unveiled temporarily outside the London Stock Exchange, intended to ignite a global conversation about the power of female leadership. The sculptor of the statue, Kirsten Visbal, commented, "I made sure to keep her features soft; she's not defiant, she's brave, proud, and strong, not belligerent."[30] This sentiment really captures my story.

Systemic layers

Many of my work colleagues would describe me as having a 'warrior spirit', which might seem at odds with a career focused on people, but I've always wanted to create workplaces where people can do their best work. Writing this story helped me explore the three layers of change: individual, group and the wider organisation that I see happening in organisations.

With the lens of gender diversity and inclusion within organisations, we can see how these systemic patterns are constantly shifting:

- The first layer: the individual: me as the human being. To what extent do the patterns and behaviours I've learnt as a female keep me small? How have my habitual patterns of being a woman, e.g. being reluctant to go for a promotion because I thought I wouldn't be good enough or failing to ask for a pay rise, affected how I've tried and sometimes failed to step into my power?
- The second layer is how we relate to others: how I show up in a group. How has my conditioning as

a woman allowed me to accept as 'normal' those everyday behaviours that undermine women as they try to work effectively together? How do I step in and access my power so that others may find theirs? How do I challenge the more subtle and everyday behaviours e.g. mansplaining, labelling assertive women 'aggressive', an inappropriate touch on the arm, all of which can get in the way of healthy relationships and dilute the power of a diverse workforce?

- The third layer is how organisations and wider society influence our lives, whether that's through gender stereotypes, unconscious bias, an education system that funnels boys one way and girls another, the expectation that women bear more responsibility for childcare and unpaid caring work, that encourage women to take lower-paying roles, part-time roles and in general more of a back seat in terms of economic independence. How has all this impacted on my ability to access my own power, to step up or in as appropriate and make sure my voice is heard?

My chapter may be about the first layer, but writing it really got me thinking about layers two and three.

As you read through my chapter, you may notice that the subject of gender is rather absent. I do wonder if that makes me a naive fool, disloyal to womanhood, or blind to the realities of the inequalities. Given the recent development of the #MeToo movement, and the courage of so many women to speak up, it doesn't feel politically correct to say that I've operated successfully in many male-dominated environments. But that's my truth, and I'm hoping that telling my story here will help me get greater insights into this journey.

Softening my fighter

I worked for News UK (previously News International) for ten years from 2006–2016. If you aren't familiar with the name, it is the publisher of *The Times, Sunday Times, The Sun* and, previously, *News of the World*. Maybe it rings a bell now? Much happened in those ten years: the emergence of free news online was changing the very nature of the business, the allegations of phone hacking (2011) eventually led to the closure of the *News of the World*, more than 20 employees were arrested, accused of having paid public officials for information, and Rupert Murdoch, the chairman, was questioned by the Culture Committee[31] in the UK Parliament about his "fitness to lead"[32] an international company. As you can imagine it was a tough and turbulent place to work, where logic and business cases were ignored in order to do what 'felt right' to those with power. It was also a place where people are deeply passionate about the place of journalism in society, super bright and talk frankly about their views especially if they disagree with you. It was never dull!

In 2013 I was appointed as HR director of *The Sun*, when it was knee-deep in a crisis. It wasn't a job I applied for, as I didn't think I was good enough. But I was told in no uncertain terms that I wasn't being asked, I was doing it. Whilst I could have seen this as a compliment, my main emotion was anger about not being given a choice. Not the most helpful response when

I probably should have been negotiating a pay rise – in other words, I didn't!

I must say, firstly, that anything I experienced pales into insignificance compared to what the journalists directly involved experienced. It took five years from the date of the first arrest to the date of the last acquittal, with individuals and their families kept in limbo and fear during that period.

Journalists at News UK were shown to have hacked phones to get stories. The lengthy police investigation took many twists and turns, and a cloud of fear hung over the newsroom both for those already affected and those who might be next. There were so many unknown aspects, but what I knew for sure was that employees were being negatively impacted by all the uncertainty. Many were facing the loss of their careers and potential financial ruin, and some the threat of a prison sentence. Individuals felt betrayed by the organisation as the police were given ever more access to company materials, in order to save the business, which was in a precarious position. Understanding this sequence of events, I felt their injustice, but rather than bury these emotions as I might have done in the past, I tried to understand them.

My warrior spirit connected deeply with the injustice, betrayal, and fear being experienced by others. On many levels this connection tested me, including around what I stood for and what it means to truly understand how to be with others and hold them with dignity when they're in pain (rather than avoiding it). As a leader, it meant acknowledging the emotions and dark places you can go to rather than being tempted to focus more simply on the practical steps to take. This meant accepting that suicide attempts were a real possibility given the stress people were under and stepping in to work with the guardian angels (other journalists who supported their colleagues, and acted as a communication channel) to understand where this was a real danger. It meant ensuring that any company communications were influenced by those who truly knew the people involved so they had heart rather than a bland corporate message. It also meant understanding the deep ripples across the rest of the organisation and looking for ways to surface this and talk about it.

My family history, and the development work I'd done, enabled me to do this work. I had to dig deep, because I was challenged by my own ethical dilemmas and my desire to fix the bigger problem. I had to accept that I wasn't trusted because I was part of the corporate animal, and that this wasn't about me. I knew that the people directly affected would never appreciate the effort being made to ease the situation for them because in all honesty we were putting 'lipstick on a pig'. There was no big solution, so we found purpose in creating small opportunities to lighten the load for all those affected. In some situations that meant looking for small life rafts to help them cope with their loss of purpose and meaning e.g. finding a charity they could work at pro-bono, a course that would help them develop new skills. For some, it meant clear communication about complex and frightening topics such as how to speak to a member of their family who wanted to understand how this had happened, and answering the question that frightened some of them the most: would we still pay them if they went to jail? But deep down I felt that, given the injustice, betrayal, and fear experienced, they deserved a team that was trying to support them through what for some were their darkest days.

The fighter

This role as HR director for *The Sun* was the end of my career at News UK, but to understand my story, we need to look at how I got there. I've been shaped by my history. Both my grandmothers singlehandedly raised families during the war, so my maternal role models were robust, firm and didn't easily express emotions. My parents encouraged me to believe in myself, and advocated that if I worked hard, I could achieve what I wanted. They sent me to school unless something was broken. As a result, my habitual pattern is to lean forward, focus on 'what's next' which means I can miss what's happening here and now. And I'm driven, stubborn, logical, comfortable with conflict and able to bury my emotions, all of which seems to resemble a fighter. Interestingly my husband describes these traits as being inherently masculine.

In my early career, these traits served me well, and on the occasions when it was suggested that other people found me rather intense or brutal, I was easily able to brush it off. In my first full-time job as a bank cashier, I remember my manager telling me that my colleagues didn't like me. My response was that I was there to do a job, not make friends. As I write this, I have a mixture of shame at the arrogance, and pride in the defiance of my retort.

I was beginning to learn that my habitual response to any sort of psychological threat was to fight back. My wake-up call that this might be a problem came in my Master's in People and Organisation Development. I joined the course full of excitement about learning new things, and energised by the intellectual challenge. Never having been to university, I was a little nervous about the amount of writing involved but my family history encouraged me to knuckle down and I told myself that if I worked hard, I would make it through.

On the first residential, one of the tutors said something that resonated with me, it was along the lines of: "You can't truly learn about people and organisations from books alone, you need to get in the f*****g pool." I'm not sure I understood the wisdom of this sage advice or what it would mean until six months later. Over the first few months, it meant facing some of my own demons and unhelpful habits about how I worked with others. I had to accept feedback from my learning set about how unpleasant it was to be on the receiving end of my fighter. My wise and patient tutor, along with my learning set, helped me to see that intellectual or 'head' learning wasn't going to help me change this fighter habit. I gradually came to understand that in order to change my habitual patterns I needed to get in touch with my own vulnerability and that this would allow me to build true partnerships, rather than taking power away from others in order for me to step into mine.

I started to explore what 'being' different might mean. Many people see development as a positive experience, but I found the opposite to be true. My master's was just the start of my journey. Although it was difficult, I continued to learn, choosing to immerse myself in both gestalt therapy and somatic coaching, along with numerous other personal development programmes. Along the way I've learned to 'manage' my fighter. The process of awakening to myself has been painful, with feelings of conscious incompetence[33] fuelling an imposter syndrome[34] because my existing ways of working were being unravelled and I hadn't yet built the capacity to work in a new way. It was often cathartic, and I cried frequently, which were tears I'd bottled up for too long. I was learning that asking for help made me feel vulnerable, but it was an important step in creating deeper connection with others. I began experimenting with how to connect with my body and, through somatic coaching with Eunice, to read the helpful data that it provided for me. I was able to loosen my armour and the tension I carried throughout my body, especially in my shoulders. Through greater connection with my physical state I became more able to understand my emotional state, slowly appreciating that my ability to shut off difficult things – by putting them in a psychological box and firmly closing the lid – wasn't healthy for me over the longer-term. I realised that by blocking my feelings I was limiting my capacity to connect with others in a meaningful way. Through somatic coaching I learnt how to stay with the physical discomfort of conflict and build my capacity to face into these things I'd previously shut off, rather than fighting back to make it stop.

Under pressure I can easily return to my fighter shape, using my head, disconnecting from my body, holding myself tightly and leaning forward, knees braced ready for battle. As I developed my capacity to stop and stand tall, centring my body and breathing deeply, I found I could create a moment for myself to make a conscious decision rather than responding instinctively. Through using my walks to and from work to centre rather than be in my head. I started off only being able to notice after the event (often accompanied by several swear words) that I'd been grabbed and wasn't in control. The daily practice of coming to feeling my body meant that I was able to catch myself in the moment. My intention was to harness the drive and courage of my fighter and develop my capacity to use it purposefully and with awareness and so fostering my warrior spirit[35]. This means I'm able to exhibit my strength but with tenderness, to challenge whilst staying in relationship with others, all while being aligned to my purpose of enabling dignity. It means integrating my fighter, my 'male' self, with my softer and more 'female' self, which is healthier for me, and also makes me a better partner for my clients. Because it means holding my power more lightly, my clients are able to get into touch with their own power.

Embodying my warrior spirit

Like many in my profession I originally stumbled into HR as a trainer and quickly found I enjoyed supporting people to develop their skills. Having worked in several industries, I'd started to get frustrated that people would leave training with great individual intentions but found their workplace or colleagues got in the way of much real change. It began to feel rather shallow because nothing significant seemed to happen as a result of my work. I could see that my real interest lay in finding broader ways to influence the workplace culture to allow people to do great work.

When I expressed this ambition to my group HR director at News UK in 2007, he told me that I needed to be at the boardroom table to influence this. I had a sense that he was inviting me to get serious. About myself and my career in HR. Getting to the boardroom table was a means of achieving my goal, not the goal in and of itself. I have a pet frustration with HR people who talk about wanting to be on the 'top table' but don't know what they'll do when they get there. Being at the boardroom table is intense, often overwhelming, full of conflicts and tensions, as McDonald's chief people officer David Fairhurst[36] argues: "When HR is in the tent, there is nowhere for the HRD to hide. It's 'deliver or wither'". But I knew why I wanted to be there and was ready for the challenge, or so I thought.

Inspired by my purpose to have a positive impact on the workplace culture, I applied for a role as Head of HR with News UK's commercial division. I knew this would be a big challenge for me and would be my first role at the 'top table'. The MD was a bear of a man with an intimidating reputation, I felt terrified and convinced myself that I probably wasn't up to the job. Sheryl Sandberg[37] argues that women hang back from these stretch roles because they worry too much about whether they have the skills for it, unlike many men, who tend to go for it regardless of their skill level. I felt compelled to apply because of my purpose and decided that I wanted to be brutally honest in the interview about my gaps and limitations as this mirrored the type of HR leader I wanted to be. I was gobsmacked when I got the role, and my desire to step into this was fuelled by having got it on my terms.

Daunted by the steep learning curve ahead of me, my imposter syndrome reared her head again. But this time I recognised what was happening and was able to be kinder to myself when I heard the critical voice in my head. I had amazing help from my team, to whom I remain eternally grateful, as I struggled with a multitude of new challenges, all of which dented my confidence. At the same time, I knew that the perception of HR was low, the general assumptions being that we were idiots or the 'fun police' or pointless (choose your own insult). So, to support my purpose of creating a culture that allowed people to do great work, I focused on using myself as an instrument of change[38] by looking for opportunities for HR to be more informal and approachable, creating a positive and helpful presence in the department rather than parachuting in when something bad happened.

As I started to understand the challenges facing the MD, my appointment made sense. The MD had seen the larger potential I could offer, beyond my operational naivety. The commercial team had recently been through a rather brutal restructure, guided by a large well-recognised consultancy. Whilst making absolute sense on paper, the consultancy had neglected the fact that the previously separate sales teams had been rivals for years, encouraged to see each other as inferior and hence were actively refusing to collaborate. New structures had been created to 'deliver' the business benefit of the new, single sales team, but no thought had been given to how to encourage the behaviours that would allow these benefits to be realised. For me, this was a great opportunity to positively influence the culture, and I threw myself into the challenge. I could see the need to change the conversations within the two teams in order to deliver the behaviour change. I chose to focus on the quality of the water in the fish tank. "Rarely do managers focus on the quality of the fishtank and what surrounds the fish: they mostly notice individual fish and become fixated on them. But if the water is toxic, the fish suffer. If there is no movement in the water, it will be deprived of life-giving oxygen. Wise owners do not blame the fish for their poor appearance or performance. They do not take the fish out from time to time to give them a spot of training, tell them to smarten up & look more lively, and then plop them back in the same dirty water. Instead they clean the tank."[39] I love this quote as a way of helping me focus on culture rather than individuals.

It was during my time as HR director that two employees died by suicide. Any HR textbook tells you about the process steps to take for an employee death, but they gloss over the shock, guilt, fear and horror that ripple through an organisation when it's a suicide. I searched for advice and guidance and found none, and so had to create meaning for myself, and for what it meant for the organisation. Because of my personal journey I knew I had to step in, and I actively encouraged conversations about how people felt, because it honoured the ending[40] we were experiencing, even if it didn't change the situation. My centring practice helped to connect with my strength to sit with the families of the employees, and other colleagues, knowing that holding their hand was part of the healing process and I tried my best to support their journey of grief, through sadness, betrayal and anger. Given my family history, however, I still felt deeply ashamed that I was unable to hold back the tears whilst telling the team about one of the deaths. However, I was told later that people truly appreciated the humanity with which I handled the situation.

These events were the catalyst for change which would focus more on understanding wellbeing across the teams and on how we could increase our collective ability to spot people struggling and find a way to help them. I was ready to fight for change, but my more collaborative and influential warrior spirit helped me convince stakeholders that, for the sake of the people working for us, we needed to invite true involvement in a new wellbeing conversation. We had to go beyond wilful blindness[41] and be prepared to see that elements such as alcohol and drugs were part of the damaging dynamic people were caught up in if we were to support people genuinely and effectively, for example.

Stepping into my power

The twists and turns of my career have inspired me and given me the courage to create my own business. I wanted to offer organisations a service that I wish had existed when I was facing extraordinary events, including support which considers that we're both human 'doings' *and* human *beings*. Extraordinary events can range in size, scale and complexity from the individual facing an imposter syndrome, the team impacted by suicide, or the organisation wanting to clean its fish tank to end a bullying culture. Through my own experience, and by focusing on my own development, I know that my warrior spirit, rather than my fighter, makes me a better coach, facilitator and consultant, more able to step into my power and empathise with those facing complex and messy problems. I'm no longer afraid to face uncomfortable truths and I no longer need to mask emotion, which means I can be truly present in helping my clients do the same thing. I can sit with them through the difficult moments and help them to see beyond their own fear or insecurity, knowing full well that they'll reap the rewards of their bravery.

Of course, this journey has triggered some of my usual habits, and I continue to be a 'work in progress'. I've faced loneliness as a entrepreneur, my imposter syndrome (again) as I try to sell my services, my conscious incompetence (again) as I face VAT returns, and I now know just how vulnerable I feel when I ask for help, something I've had to do more often than I'd like. But as I ride this rollercoaster, I can draw on my warrior spirit, knowing the strength, courage and power that it gives me, understanding that I have choice in how I use it.

I hope my story has helped you consider and explore the multiple layers that can be involved as we find our voice and step into our power as women, beyond the much-discussed elements of motherhood and childcare. When I was asked to write this chapter, my first response was of deep terror at putting myself out in the world and being seen by others. I invite you to think about how you might become your most powerful self, acknowledging the fear, terror even, that that might involve you facing into.

What the research revealed...

Research theme two: The power of presence and aligning our actions with our purpose.

When we turn our attention inwards and deeply connect with what we care about, we embody an authentic leadership presence, one that cultivates trust and embodies greater ease and connection. When we align what we care about, our purpose, with our external actions, we're seen as believable and someone people want to move forward with, engage with and follow. More importantly we feel confident in who we are and our capacity to make things happen. Many of the women leaders described how getting present enabled them to speak their truth, to take authentic action and to hold a bigger space for whatever was unfolding in the wider system. One client, a female director from the financial industry, told me, "Identifying my purpose was transformational for me, it has enabled me to find the courage to say what I think and to move into action." "My purpose is always with me; it shapes my action. I now put myself forward for things I would have moved away from previously," said another.

Laurence Hollobon, who at the time was the European HR Director for Bel, said, "Being truly in my power comes from having a sense of purpose. When I truly embody my power, I am able to create an environment where others can be better at what they do and produce more meaningful work."

When a leader embodies her purpose, she can access the courage and the confidence to speak her truth in an honest and meaningful way.

An invitation to practise – Centring practice

Carrie's story illustrates for us just what becomes possible when we turn our attention inwards, listen deeply to what really matters to us; there's a resonance that gently moves us forward. When we learn to centre, we're more present, we have more choice, more agency and, better equipped to take care of what matters to us.

Here's a centring practice for you to try…

Stand, with your arms relaxed at your side and your feet hip width apart. Align yourself so that your head is directly over your shoulders, your shoulders over your hips, hips over your knees and your knees over the mid-point of your feet.

Turn your attention inwards, tune into your sensations, notice temperature, where you feel warm or cold, pressure, where you feel contracted, where you feel relaxed, where you *don't* feel. Notice where your breath is, high in your chest or low in your belly? And what is your mood? No judgement, just noticing what is happening in you right now.

Now take three deep breaths and with each breath drop your attention to your centre, a few centimetres below your belly button. This is your centre of gravity.

From here we centre in four dimensions.

First centre in length – all the way down to your lower body, while simultaneously lengthening up, occupying your full height. Balancing the two halves of the body, bottom and top. Settling down and lengthening up, centring in your full length and inside of that centring in your dignity, your self-worth.

Then centre in your width where we balance the left and right sides of our body. Letting yourself unfurl, unfold, filling out across your shoulders, hips, knees and feet, noticing where you end and the world starts. Width is the dimension of belonging, of taking up your space in the world.

Next centre in depth, third dimension, front to back, back to front. Take your attention to your back, the space behind you, reminding yourself of all that has brought you to this moment, your lived experiences. Imagine all of that supporting you in this moment. Come into your inside, let yourself feel your lungs expanding as you breathe. And then coming all the way through to your front body, ready to face into whatever is ahead of you, today, the months and years to come.

Finally, the fourth dimension, centring around what matters, what you care about, just say that to yourself and as you do let it fill the three dimensions of length, width and depth. And let it resonate from your centre.

Ask yourself:

- What's your mood now, one or two words that capture your mood in this moment?
- What do you care about?
- What's possible for you if you align your actions with what you care about?

Alison Lazerwitz is the general counsel for the Swarovski Group. This family-run business was founded in 1895. Alongside her global role, Alison is also a member of the leadership team for the finance and administration group whose story of leading transformative change I told in my first book, Embodying Authenticity. Since then, Alison has continued to cultivate her leadership, while also giving back by mentoring female leaders who are at the beginning of their leadership career.

In her chapter, Alison demonstrates that by understanding her own history she was able to reveal the patterns that no longer served her or needed managing in new ways. She illustrates how we often make decisions based on an inner need, a yearning, feeling or sensation which we subsequently rationalise – and that if we could tune into these sensations earlier and with more compassion, we could make choices that are about what's truly important to us. As a lawyer, Alison is a well-practised advocate for others – her journey shows us how she had to find a way to advocate for herself in order to step more fully into her power.

Chapter Four

Discovering my courage in the white spaces

Alison Lazerwitz
Introduction

I often find myself at a business school in front of a group of eager (always younger) colleagues giving a talk that is loosely associated with leadership and the challenges of being a woman leader. There are two things I've learned from these talks. The first is that the audiences are receptive to hear my story and what I have to say, based on my track record of achieving success as a woman in senior executive positions in global businesses for more than 30 years, and that I have a certain amount of credibility to talk about many of the same headwinds that young women (and men) face today. The second is that opening a window on who I am, and the family and cultural forces that shaped me, guides me through these sessions. I invariably close the talk with a cautionary piece of advice: my choices are my own, and the only certainty I possess is that there is no one road map: something working for one person is no indication that it'll work for anyone else.

With that in mind, I found that exploring certain 'white spaces' in my CV, looking back on these decisions and making sense of my choices have contributed to a deeper understanding of who I have become, and why. This exploration has helped me to celebrate my successes and forgive myself for setbacks. While it would be easy to define myself by what I've accomplished in my career by reading the headings and the first lines of my CV, what I find to be the better insights into how I've grown to meet the challenges of a career and my own personal development are found in the 'in-betweens', in the choices that shaped me: the white spaces. How and why did I make the decisions that I did and what do these say about my growth as a woman in business? I've been so fortunate to have support and guidance from a remarkable group of women, and I gain strength from the knowledge that we all benefit from those around us reaching their potential, especially the young women I've had the fortune to meet along my career. If in some way my story and my discoveries help others reach their own potential, then I've helped build the pyramid of women leadership.

I grew up in a family and culture where achievement was possible, so long as you worked for it. We were taught to know the difference between entitlement and earning achievement. I am the oldest of three children and I have two younger brothers. We grew up in the shadow of New York City, the ultimate expression of American optimism and possibilities. I flourished in comfort, not wealth, and in a loving environment where possibilities were to be cherished and success within reach. While both my parents were products of the traditional values and role models of the times, both my father and mother instilled in me the chance to be different. My father, a dentist, was a traditional bread-winner who cherished his role as the head of the household but saw in me the potential to break out of the mold of being raised to be a wife and mother. My mother was a fearless homemaker who taught me by example how contributions to the family come in a variety of packages as she controlled the family dynamic as my father's equal. She never considered her job anything less than on a par with my father. Both my parents gave me, in their separate ways, the space to dream and not to be constrained by stereotypes. That being said, as the oldest child my natural tendency is to please and to meet others' expectations as a way to define my own success. These competing forces play a recurring role in my life's choices.

An example of my father's influence on me (and how I continue to be driven by my very early experiences) was a talk we had over brunch in New York City one Sunday. It was just the two of us, and my dad told me that I was special, that I should do whatever I thought I needed to do, and THEN think about getting married. I was not yet 12 years old. (My father and I still joke that I must have taken this advice seriously, as many decades later, I am still not married.) I'd internalized external definitions of success and also had 'permission' to listen to what I wanted to achieve, disregard others' opinions and find my own path. It's only recently that I recognized this gift as an internal dialogue to explore alternatives and an invitation to listen to my innermost thoughts and feelings.

The foundation of my family, the tapestry of experiences around New York City, strong women role models and the achievability of success, shape me to this day. One set of experiences that left an indelible mark happened each summer from the time I was ten until I turned 15. Each year I went to residential camp for eight weeks. These childhood experiences are as much a part of who I am as the bedroom where I slept until I went away to college. Summer camp opened my eyes to peers who came from wealth and privilege, it introduced me to the magic of the Berkshire mountains in the summer with Tanglewood (music), Jacob's Pillow (dance) and Williamstown Playhouse (theater) that was a treasure trove to a teenager. Most of all, this experience crystallized for me a self-image I grapple with to this day: a slightly plump outsider who was never part of the 'cool' gang, but who became the confidante of the coolest girl in the group if she had a problem or needed a safe space to express doubts. There were dances after evening activity several times a week, and each summer I'd dread these events, as I was often not asked to dance (we still waited for boys to ask) or was asked by the nerdiest guy around. I was never sure which was worse.

Growing up and finding myself in positions of increasing authority, there's always, somewhere, this dichotomy: the girl who was sought after for her advice and perspective and who gained some confidence from this position, and on the other hand someone who wasn't cool, and not fashionably attractive. Both sides accompanied me through my teens, my university years and into my professional life. And I've had quite the professional ride. I graduated from the University of Virginia with an undergraduate degree in the humanities then went on to law school at the same university. I started my legal career with a prestigious Philadelphia law firm (and I owe my legal skills and my admiration for the legal profession to the men and women who trained me at this firm). I then went on to legal positions with companies located in Pennsylvania in the US, Paris, France and ultimately Zurich, Switzerland. My jobs have included litigation associate, associate general counsel, general counsel, chief legal officer, and executive vice president. These titles and positions don't define who I am; those descriptions would include significant other, sister, daughter, friend, aunt, godmother, and fairy godmother.

How the two sides of me merge into one, and how they surface through certain choices I made, create the foundation from which I celebrate what I've achieved and who I've become.

Ending the habit of starting a sentence with an apology

I'm writing this chapter from the security of a highly visible legal position for a global manufacturing and retail industry leader. I'm the head of an international legal team of skilled professionals that literally spans the globe and I have access to the most senior management decisions in an ever-changing dynamic business environment. I operate in an environment of trust and confidence and have been in Zurich, Switzerland, as an expatriate for more than eight years. I've adapted to the new culture that a new country and a new industry brings. Which leads me to an event that happened almost five years ago and has had a lasting impression on the person and the leader that I try to be today.

The management team that I'm a part of is comprised of all functional department heads that report to the same member of the executive board. These colleagues include the leaders of all back-office functions, such as operations, finance, human resources, IT, procurement and legal. We were embarking on a leadership journey for our senior leaders and our boss decided that this transformation needed to start with us as the senior leadership team. We brought in an external consultant and facilitator (Eunice) to engage with us in a series of conversations that were at the same time highly personal and also collective. Early in the process, after a particularly difficult team session, Eunice asked me if she could privately offer some feedback. While the politically correct answer is to say yes (and I did), I wasn't very keen to hear anything, and certainly not anything that would cast aspersions on my ability to effectively collaborate and contribute to the team development. What Eunice asked me was so unexpected and so profound that I remember it like it was yesterday. She asked me if I knew how much power I held in the room, and if I did, why did I start what were otherwise insightful and important contributions with an apology? Why was I beginning my observations with statements like, "I may not know what I am talking about but…" or "I may be off base in saying this but…"? Eunice asked me to think about where this was coming from and then without skipping a beat, or waiting for me to respond, she offered her own advice.

She suggested that while I was figuring out the 'why', I should consider owning the place that I already have in the room and stop apologizing for being 'smart.' She suggested that it's very hard to be small and doubt your own voice if you can summon strength from being centered and grounded. She offered the following: before I speak, make sure that I'm fully conscious of my physical presence and that I'm in the moment. Put both feet on the floor, sit back and tall in my chair, and then open my mouth. She promised that from this physical presence, I'd pause before I retreated to the habit of starting a sentence with an apology or another self-deprecating remark. Of course, she was right and the change of physical presence acted as a trigger for shifts in my emotional state. While it wasn't instantaneous, over time I found a way to practice some new habits. When I was involved in a conversation (and in my line of work, many of them are contentious), I tried (not always successfully) to pause before speaking, gain strength from being in the moment and to get in touch with what my body was telling me. I learned to make a conscious decision about whether I'd lead from a position of power or apology.

Much later Eunice and I had several conversations about the 'why' behind the behavior and the various threads in my life which contribute to me being a successful and confident leader while at the same time doubting my talents (the teenager who wasn't asked to dance in summer camp).

These conversations inevitably led to a series of reflections on choices I made, and what the choices tell me about who I've become. Three key decisions helped me to put the threads together:

- Leaving my first job and getting off the partnership track
- Rejecting a safe job offer and moving to Paris
- Quitting a job without having another one

What emerged was an inner conviction or strength that I relied upon to choose to move towards opportunities where I could thrive and move away from situations that prevented this from happening. What also became apparent is that although I didn't have the vocabulary or the insights to identify what was happening at the time, the trend was clear. I'd somehow managed to find the courage to strip away conventional thinking and listen to what my heart was telling me. Trusting your own inner voice takes courage and from that place, we're then able to help others hear their own voices and find their own sources of strength.

Choice: leave the law firm and go in-house

When you grow up as I did, in a house of achievers and possibilities, it was second nature to strive for success. Good grades, ranking in the top percentile in your class, admittance to a prestigious college, law school, or law firm. It was a pattern I was comfortable with (even when stressed or insecure). And it was a game I was winning. While there were the inevitable disappointments and setbacks, the trajectory was mostly positive and up. Some of this confidence came from my New York background and an era in the United States where the idea was that 'women could have it all'. I believed it. We could be ambitious, smart, consummate professionals and loving wives and mothers all at the same time. While I wasn't hugely successful in the social arena (the outsider from camp was omni-present), I thought there'd be time for it all and I was gaining strength from the increasing feeling that I was a good student and then later a good lawyer. I'd be able to use my professional expertise as a springboard for other successes. At this time in my life I was relying on my intellect to get me through. I hadn't yet developed the 'muscle' to also listen to how my decisions made me feel.

This is the backdrop for my first 'white space' choice: the decision to take myself out of the running and leave the law firm before the decision was taken to 'make me a partner.' For those of you who aren't familiar with the definition of success in law firms, it was fairly simple back then: you joined as an associate (an employee) and you worked tirelessly based on others' expectations, and then 'magically', after a certain number of years, you were voted into (or out of) the ranks of the partnership. The criteria were somewhat (altogether) opaque and completely subjective, and as far as I could tell, I was on track.

Then something happened, and it turned out not to be a unique event in my life of decision-making. I was about to start the first trial where I was the lead (and only) attorney. In the middle of organizing my thoughts for the pre-trial and trial hearings, a nagging question would not go away: Did I want to be a partner and devote myself to this calling?

This question was terrifying. I'd never dared to ask it before. Instead, I'd been obsessed by a different question: Would they make me a partner and what did I have to do to ensure that I would win? On the morning on my way to court, I'd consider how much I wanted to be selected, and how great it would be to 'make partner.' On my way back home at the end of the day I'd ask myself the opposite: did I like what I was doing as a litigator and did I want to do this for the rest of my life? (Binary choices and thoughts were easier then when I had not yet reached 30 and choices seemed to be much clearer.)

This was the first time I'd dared to consider what it was about the job and making partner that worked for me. What made me happy and who did I want to be? On the one hand, status mattered (and still matters) to me and I had to be honest with myself that I wanted the recognition of having succeeded in the conventional sense. It was more than that though, as I also wanted to fulfill others' expectations: those of the partners who'd mentored me, of my parents who understood that partnership was a sign of success and stability and, frankly, my own definition of success. On the other hand, there was the growing realization that while I could develop the skills necessary to be a successful litigator, I did not love the fight. I did not come alive in the courtroom and I did not thrive on winning at all costs. Instead, I recognized that what I loved about my job was learning about a client's business, figuring out the problem and being part of the solution. The fact was that once I turned the question around and asked what would ultimately allow me to be most true to myself and my strengths, the answer was not what I'd expected: I needed to move on.

Asking these questions led me to make a decision on a set of criteria I hadn't previously considered: what would feel best for me? The logical conclusion based on my upbringing and world around me was to stay and be a partner. However, those 'other' considerations changed my career path back then and have accompanied me through later decisions: where would I shine best, where did my heart and not my head take me, where could I feel the most fulfilled? After some recent coaching sessions with Eunice and an introduction to new vocabulary, I can now see these questions in terms of how could I step into my own power? But at the time I didn't have that vocabulary, I was dealing with feelings and the choice between being afraid of going off the chosen path and focusing on my greatest chance of happiness.

What has sustained me, and helped me with future decisions, was a need to find the answer to the question, 'what would it take for me to be at my best?' I left the law firm in advance of being nominated to be a partner and made a turn in my career to becoming a general counsel. The competing feelings of strength on one hand and the potential for making a mistake on the other led me to reflect on how we all make choices to navigate through uncertainty. A theme developed for me that may be helpful for women who are thinking about their management potential: be clear on what's beneath the surface of our own decisions so that we can stand up for our choices and help others in path-finding through their own. Path-finding for others is not a reason in and of itself to do something, but it has become an important part of my leadership experiences. I continue to be humbled by the attention that my decision to leave the law firm created at the time, and how I was admired for being 'brave.' It's a responsibility I've cherished to this day.

Choice: leave the US and go to Paris

My decision away from the law firm partnership track and to the life of an in-house legal counsel led me to a series of companies, first in Philadelphia and then in Allentown, Pennsylvania. I learned the trade and the art of working with senior managers and a board of directors from the bottom up. The company in Allentown was managed by a tight group of colleagues who became, over time, more like a family than a group of co-workers. Into this dynamic came the reality that the owners were selling the company. The importance of the new owner for my career was all too clear: my position in the new combined organization would be redundant and I'd lose my job. I did all that I could to support the sale process. A French company bought 'my' company. The French company's international headquarters were located in Paris and the US subsidiary was many times bigger than the Allentown company it had just acquired.

In the course of the months following the sale, the acquiring management team was tasked with meeting with their counterparts in 'my company' to agree on an integration plan for each division or function. The legal team was no exception. I met with my counterpart and we first sorted out our respective teams and then it was time to negotiate my position. I was ready. We went through the formalities of my counterpart praising my abilities and announcing the party line that the company was eager for me to find a place in the new organization. I was flattered but something made me hesitate. It would have been safe to accept a position in the new organization, even if it didn't fit with what I wanted to do. But something stopped me, and it's not an overstatement to say that this decision changed the direction of my life. Literally.

The same themes that had surfaced years earlier with my decision to leave the law firm came back. I had tremendous respect for my counterpart in the new organization and his talents and experience clearly made him the logical choice for the head of the combined legal teams. At the same time, I had an idea that I wouldn't be happy watching someone in the leadership role when I would be playing a supporting one. I was in touch with my feelings enough to recognize that my ego would not allow me to be content in the new organization. I 'knew' that the first time he was called into the CEO's office for a consultation or attended a senior leadership team meeting (and I didn't) that I'd resent it and him. I was not posturing when I thanked him for the compliments and the vote of confidence to stay, but I told him that I wouldn't be 'happy' in a subordinate role since I'd already been the head of the legal department. This wasn't what he wanted to hear but he completely understood. There was an awkward silence as we then needed to discuss severance and timing, and then, out of nowhere, with no forethought or planning on my part, I said, "But what about the Paris headquarters? Don't you need an American lawyer in the French headquarters more than you need another American lawyer in the US subsidiary?" To this day I have no idea where this came from other than the certainty that I wouldn't be happy in the US subsidiary and that an opportunity to try something completely new was more appealing than what I felt would be a dead-end. This meeting plays out in my head like a movie scene: I see myself volunteering to move to Paris and the man sitting across from me looks up incredulously and says, "You would move to Paris?" My response is straight out of a movie script: "I'm living in Allentown, Pennsylvania... Allentown, Paris, Allentown, Paris... Hell yes."

This conversation highlights another time in my life's choices where the voices from my heart were louder than the intellectual voices in my head. While at the time, my suggestion to move to France appeared to have come out of nowhere, it actually came from a sense of identity. Following a path to find out how to maximize my strengths, and not get stuck in a job that wasn't fulfilling, was at the core of my idea that the new company could offer me a position in Paris. It was an idea that had been resting on the shoulders of many decisions and hopes that had been building up since I knew that the company was going to be sold. It was a form of self-preservation that I felt, rather than knew conceptually.

Six months later I was on an Air France flight to Paris, with a one-way ticket in my hand. As I retell the story (and I have told this story many times, trying as hard as I can to emphasize the luck involved and the complete lack of planning or skill), the theme that resonates is that I really hadn't thought through the implications of my outburst beforehand. I had no idea what I was getting into but who wouldn't want to live in Paris? I thought of it as a dream, with no clear path of how to fulfill the desire. I managed my fear by thinking through worst-case scenarios. I'd live in Paris for a few years, soak in the magic of living abroad, and then return to the US. Going on an adventure to one of the most glamorous European capitals was romantic, exciting, and completely beyond my experiences. I'd lived up until then with a personal mantra: I obviously had made mistakes, but I didn't want to live with regrets. Regrets drag us down and pull us backward. I'd instinctively felt this and now I had a chance to live it. I could only imagine that if I didn't grab the opportunity to live and work in Paris it would be something I'd always regret. The inverse could not be true: Would I ever regret going to Paris and finding out if I could pull it off? The answer was a resounding no. That day on the Air France flight was almost 17 years ago… I've lived in Europe ever since.

Choice: leave a job without having another one

Living in Paris and being able to internalize that I, in some small way, can call Paris 'home' is a wonder of my life that I'll never fully comprehend. For eight years, my daily commute involved turning a corner and seeing the Eiffel Tower. No matter how grey the day, no matter what had happened (or not) at work, I tried to keep the magic in perspective. A girl from Fair Lawn, New Jersey, ordered croissants in French every Sunday from the same *boulangerie*, rented a house in Provence from the same family every year, and considered the Eiffel Tower a neighborhood attraction. I tried not to feel entitled to the experience and not to take it for granted.

Living as an expatriate in Europe fulfilled all the challenges and experiences that one could imagine and many that I couldn't. I often recount this part of my career history with as much humor and self-deprecation as I can for this is true: it wasn't courage that propelled me across the Atlantic, it was naivete. What others saw as courage, I internalized as listening to that inner voice which was propelling me forward. That isn't to say I regret it, not for one minute. But the things I didn't know could fill many books: I knew enough of the language to be dangerous (or as I say, my French was passable tourist French, menus, wine lists and directions to the bathroom). I completely underestimated the French certainty that Paris (and not New York) was the center of the universe, and that not knowing a language and a culture will deprive you of one of the essential tools I had previously taken for granted, the ability to undercut or decrease tension with humor.

I learned everything about being an international lawyer during my tenure in-house in Paris. I started out in the legal department as international counsel (a title we made up because there was no job description). During my first years in Paris, the business environment changed and the headquarters location had an increasing need for a lawyer who had American training. The legal department was reorganized and I took on added responsibilities as the first chief legal officer of the international group. I was involved in transactions and activities that a year or two before I wouldn't have known how to spell, let alone provide legal advice and counselling. It was terrifying, exciting, overwhelming and remarkably fulfilling all at the same time.

The work was fascinating, the pace was exhausting and I was surprisingly comfortable in an international environment where I developed a talent for aligning diverse perspectives and bringing cultures together. I had a few coaches and some sponsors, but most of the time I was on my own to figure it out. While I didn't report directly to the CEO, he'd spent a large part of his career in the US and he took an informal interest in my success as a US transplant in a very French company. He and I met on a very informal basis, usually once a year for dinner where we talked off the record. These meetings were a training ground for me to develop skills in providing counsel through informal conversations, and the invaluable ability to enable others to find their answers with open-ended questions and empathy.

The pace of living as an ex-pat, and the loneliness/isolation you feel without the safety net of 'home', is hard to describe if you haven't experienced it. It's not something you articulate often, as you get little sympathy for living abroad in a city as glamorous as Paris. So, the realization that the internal environment of the organization wasn't allowing me to thrive was a very long time in coming. There was so much to learn, so much that was unfamiliar, that finding my voice and my 'center' was always in doubt.

Gradually, however, it became clear to me (and those loved ones around me) that the conflicts I was having at work were broader than cultural differences. The things that I thought were my strengths, the characteristics that I held dear as being part of my core – bringing others around the table together, having insights but being comfortable if others took credit if they thought they were good ideas, and above all a sense of laughter and joy –

weren't appreciated by those I worked with and were devalued by my senior management. At the time I felt this disconnect more than I could articulate it. Then, one night, at one of the informal dinners with the CEO, in response to a fairly routine question, "So, how are you doing?" I cracked. Before I knew what was happening, I said that I was losing the sense of who I was and that in the current situation I wasn't able to be myself. I literally said out loud that I thought I was in danger of "losing Alison". I hadn't planned on saying these things, I'm not sure I had even admitted them to myself before that night. As soon as I'd said them, the sentences lay on the table, along with the baguette and the butter. There was no recrimination in the CEO's response, there was compassion, and understanding. He told me that no job was worth losing yourself. There was nothing else to say. Once I'd lent my voice to the reality, there was no stepping back. For the first time in my career I lay the groundwork to resign without having a new job in place. Other circumstances were involved, of course, no decision is based on a single event or without complications, but that dinner conversation in a Paris bistro started a series of events that found me in Paris, without a job, eight years and five months after I'd arrived. What I can tell you about that time is that lawyers are notoriously control freaks (I fit that description to a T) and that I didn't do 'free fall' well. I worried about the future and how to best orchestrate a new job from the time I woke up until the time I went to bed. What I never questioned was the wisdom of getting out of a situation where I felt I was getting lost and couldn't bring my best self forward.

While looking for a job was neither easy or natural, before the end of the year, I was offered a general counsel position in Switzerland.

Going forward: honoring my voice

There are countless decisions and personal interactions that form who we are, and I've no idea whether these four events are the most important or representative of anything other than four white spaces on my CV. I know that in defining who I am and who I want to be, it's important to continuously recognize the gifts that others have brought to me, and the serendipity of decisions and opportunities.

I'm not sure that there's one moment or one particular experience that has shaped me. My father tells the story that my nursery school teacher commented on the fact that as a four year old, I was already making sure that everyone was included in the daily games, that all the children in the class had the right pencils and equipment, and that I acted as the hostess for the conversations over cookies and milk. I don't remember this, but my dad does. He says I haven't changed. We're all kaleidoscopes of experiences, decisions and the growing recognition that all of it shapes who we are and want to be.

I've always felt lucky to be a woman. I believe that as women we have the freedom to go outside boundaries and continuously adapt, while at the same time, we share an affinity for silent strength and trust in our feelings. We can benefit from the fact that others may underestimate us, delight people with our ability to succeed and be stronger than we even thought possible. In recognizing the gifts that have been given to me, paying back and forward isn't a choice, it's a responsibility.

What the research revealed...

Research theme three: Accessing power from within, listening to our intuitive self.

In a world where we're more connected globally than we ever were before and where technology is evolving at a faster pace than we perhaps could have ever imagined, organisations are beginning to move away from traditional hierarchies to becoming networked organisations that require leaders to be more conscious, more connected and more consequent. In this changing context the need for a 'feminine' energy in senior leadership is critical. Tricia Hitmar, Director of Talent GVSE, Cisco, spoke about how she's able to influence others as part of navigating a large organisational system by drawing on 'power from within', "I have to dig deep and access my intuitive power." Or as Sandy DeFelice, who we met earlier, shared, "I draw on my instinctual power a lot even though in a male-dominated environment drawing on instinct can be easily dismissed in favour of thoroughly thinking something through." What Sandy is pointing us to is what many of the women I spoke to said – that in a world where rationality is king and getting things done is privileged, they're afraid to move from their intuitive sense. And so they don't. However, when we learn to turn our attention inwards and listen to our deeper selves we can not only connect with our innermost truth but also bring our true voices to the workplace. It doesn't have to be an either/or, but an integration of both the rational and the intuitive.

When a leader embraces her instinctual power, she's able to take risks that honour her vision and longing.

81

An invitation to practise – Sitting practice

In Alison's story she shares with us how, in those moments when she knew she needed to move towards opportunities where she could thrive, she was able to listen to her inner voice and access her instinctual power. Alison talked about how being in the practice of centring and focusing inwards helped build her capacity to sense, feel and access her intuitive self.

How else might we cultivate our intuitive self? How do we make space and time to connect with our aliveness, to our core way of being, our whole selves so we might feel a sense of agency? Sitting practice, meditation, mindfulness practice – whatever way we choose to call it – invites us to cultivate our intuitive selves.

Find a place to sit where you feel at ease and resourced and try this for yourself:

- As you sit, feel your back in the chair, straighten your spine and sit upright
- Let your breath drop so it is low and rhythmic
- Let your eyes close and focus your attention on your breath, noticing your in-breath and out-breath
- When you notice your mind drifting into thought or you find yourself distracted away from your breath, then gently invite yourself to come back – come back to your breath.

You may like to take this on as a daily practice – sitting each day for ten minutes.

We come into this world as inherently genuine and authentic human beings. Over time we layer on conditioning that generates those all too familiar automatic responses. When we sit, we can remove the veil that obscures our authentic self, opening up a channel for us to be in direct relationship with who we are. In learning to pay attention in this way, we interrupt our habitual conditioning and begin to feel into the voice of that deeper, wiser part of ourselves.

Meet Lucia Adams, a thought leader in the field of digital transformation, who at the time of writing had just begun a five-month assignment as the managing editor at i newspaper.

I came to know Lucia when she was completing her post-graduate coaching qualification. I facilitated a session which introduced the somatic coaching methodology. This resonated with Lucia and not long after she asked me to be her coach. Lucia and I worked on deepening her capacity as a leader as she moved from a high-profile corporate role at The Times newspaper to building her own business. As Lucia explains in her story, she's not unused to making bold moves but as she stepped into the unknown yet again, she became aware that her old ways of working were no longer serving her. If she were truly to find her own power, she needed to deconstruct the emotional patterns, adaptive strategies and automatic reactions that were getting in the way of her developing her leadership and her business.

Lucia's chapter is an invitation to all of us as leaders to see what becomes possible when we are able to routinely interrupt old habits and patterns and align our actions to what we value, what we care about. Lucia shares with us how working in the digital arena invited her to engage in her own development as a leader, learn to lead others while also creating her own framework for leading digital transformation.

Chapter Five

Stepping into the unknown

Lucia Adams
Leadership in an unpredictable world

The tyres of my bicycle crunch over frost and grit as I lean into the gentle, protracted incline on the last leg of my daily commute to the *i* newspaper office in High Street Kensington. It's daybreak – the cold biting my cheeks like little daggers. I've already traversed some of London's most dazzling landmarks: past the London Eye, over the Thames, a nod to Big Ben, an inquiring glance at The Houses of Parliament, a quick marvel at whatever's unfolding outside Buckingham Palace – the final stretch taking me along Hyde Park where mounted horse riders stroll languidly – incongruous alongside the rush of cars, motorbikes, buses and joggers – all powering towards their morning commitments.

I'm powering too. It's my first day back in the office after spending two days with Eunice's embodied leadership group in the Hampshire countryside and just 12 weeks since I took a five-month assignment at i as managing editor – a role that spans a wide remit: print innovation, digital strategy, organisational development, as well as managing the finances and dealing with legal and IPSO issues. I've joined the paper at an exciting time: 10 years after its inception, *i* has proven wrong those who doubted it. It's transformed from a disruptive loss-making start-up, to a highly profitable news brand with bright prospects. Consistent editorial excellence and commercial success persuaded DMGT to buy *i* for £49.6m two weeks after I started. It's been quite a learning curve: getting to grips with the business while also working with the editor in chief and leadership team to mould the paper's future ambitions and strategy.

As I ride to work, my head is operating at two tempos: a staccato 'task mode', punctuated by each press of my pedals, ticking off all the operational things I need to sort that week; the other, legato mode, is expansive as I contemplate the long-term plans I'm supporting the senior team to develop. I'm puzzling over how to find the right balance between the immediate demands of the job and making space to focus on the long-term.

The morning blue-pink sky isn't yet warm enough to burn away the mist that cloaks The Serpentine lake. Like my three sons who are still at home tucked up in bed, Hyde Park remains blanketed under the fog, refusing to rise and join the hurly burly of another day in the city. This reluctance to rush into the day gives me pause for thought. It invites me to slow down, centre myself and remember my learning from the previous couple of days. The space to slow down is there already if I'd care to listen to it call.

I'm swollen with the insights I've gained working with Eunice's action learning group. Once again, I'm facing into a familiar pattern of striving – driving myself hard. The past two days have challenged me to settle my nervous system – to be more present to myself, others and the wider system – in order to more skilfully move through the twists, turns and ambiguities that characterise so much of business in this epoch of accelerating change. I remember how it feels to have my ground, choosing how I show up, stepping into my own power.

Evolving through digital: stepping into the void

My growth as a leader mirrors the evolution of digital. When I first started out in the working world, it was 1997; I typed my university dissertations on basic word processors and went to the library to use the 'internet'; Google wouldn't launch until 1998, so reference books were your best bet for getting quality information. People still got their news in printed newspapers. In the decade that followed, my digital graduation could be seen as forward-thinking; but in reality, digital was often considered as the poor cousin in legacy businesses. The dot.com revolution was making people sit up and notice – but in the wake of that bubble bursting, online teams were seen as second-class parts of the business. 'Online' was often seen as frivolous and irrelevant, a distraction from the 'real work'. It was in this context, in 2006, that I was offered a job at Times Online.

By this time Google was well established and Facebook was just starting to go mainstream. Advertising revenue was declining at news organisations. *The Times* had had a web presence since 1999, but there was a growing awareness that the future of newspapers was under threat, and the paper needed to take online more seriously. My inspiring, championing boss, Anne Spackman, moved to be editor in chief at Times Online, signalling that online would be key to the newspaper's future, and she asked me to join the team. The job offer was one I battled over. My head was telling me that staying on the paper was the 'sensible' thing to do – the neat career path, the low-risk option. I was afraid that by stepping into the online world, I would somehow lose my way. On the other hand, I could see that the appointment of my highly respected boss was going to change all this. I took a leap into the void, as Joseph Campbell[42] describes it, a space of not knowing; I accepted the job.

It was a pivotal moment for me, I felt called to step out of my comfort zone and into the world of digital. And at the same time, I was leaving behind everything that was familiar to me. It's easy with the benefit of hindsight to see this as a canny move – it's only now that we can see how digital has evolved from a low-status side gig to the most pressing challenge faced by every industry. At the time, it felt like a calling that required me to take a leap of faith.

This leap would ask me to adapt in ways I couldn't have imagined; learning how to respond to this constantly changing environment invited me to evolve as a leader. This meant learning new skills – but it also required a different sort of commitment: a commitment to continuous learning, getting comfortable with not knowing all the answers, holding the space for others so they felt able to come on the journey with us. Being at the cutting edge of digital meant that the answers to the business problems we would be working through weren't to be found in any textbook or training programme. The teams tasked with building a new future for the newspaper were inventing every day. It was a process of constant discovery and experimentation. And while this filled me with excitement, it was also a test of my old patterns: moving into a field where I wasn't an expert triggered me to work extra hard to master this new world. Often my inner critic would find me lacking, so I drove myself harder and harder – I was constantly reading, researching, meeting new people, and striving to be at the top of my game.

This wasn't always a healthy balance: it took the intervention of a work friend for me to see this striving pattern was embedded deeply in me. It was 2008 and I was heavily pregnant with my first child; my colleague stopped by my desk on his way home one evening. It was another long day for me working late into the night – a habit he'd noticed. Concerned for my welfare, he suggested that I'd need to rethink this way of working. It had got me far, through big career changes and promotions, but striving had become my crutch, and it started to dawn on me that it came at a cost to my wellbeing. But how could I be successful without it? Somehow the consequences of working so hard, in spite of its high cost, seemed worth it. It's a habit I am periodically forced to reassess.

Learning to listen to my inner compass

I'm familiar with big leaps into the unknown. I'd opted to change schools in the sixth form – something that simply no one ever did in my small Northern Irish hometown. It was bold, and I came in for criticism as a result. I'd also taken a career leap in my late 20s – media was my second career; I'd started out in retail having joined a fast-track management development programme at Kingfisher. While my time there was an amazing education and

89

powerful experience working across many different parts of the organisation, it felt like there was something missing.

Over many months I became increasingly dissatisfied. Those feelings grew to a crescendo until I could no longer ignore them. It was terrifying. I knew that what I was doing was making me deeply unhappy, but I had no idea what I should be doing instead. My overwhelming urge was to suppress my instinct: my conditioning had taught me to ignore what I wanted. I was supposed to 'get on with it' and 'be grateful for what I had'. When I spoke to colleagues, friends, and family about my dilemma they tried to convince me of the folly in leaving a well-paid job with great prospects to propel myself into the unknown. And when they asked me what I would do next, I had no answer.

While it was difficult to recognise at the time, my need to 'transform' was an insight into the battle between my innate 'wisdom' about what I was meant to offer the world, and my conditioning that taught me to ignore what I wanted deep down. Just like the decision to change schools and careers, moving to Times Online was stepping outside of a linear paradigm. The rigid context of the old world of neat career paths clashed with my own evolutionary process of discovery. I started to realise that I'd learnt to suppress the instinctive part of myself – to privilege the intellect over instinct.

Looking back, each time I've committed to a new course of action, it's challenged me to move away from accepting the conventional view. It's been an internal battle between 'just getting on with it', staying within the confines of the status quo, toward developing my inner pathfinder and becoming more visible. Now I can see how these decisions constituted moves towards discovering my purpose. My ongoing work is centred on cultivating that inner voice of wisdom, while quietening my reaction of fear, in order to stay in tune with my emerging purpose and ultimately bring my 'power' into the world. Unbeknownst to me, the invitation to join Times Online would be a significant catalyst in deconstructing some of my reactive tendencies that no longer served me in this new digital world.

Stepping into my power: living the challenge

It was 2009, I'd just returned from my first maternity leave at *The Times*. A difficult time for me as, like many returning mums, my confidence had taken a nosedive. I was working in a highly competitive 24/7 news environment, juggling career, childcare and home life. The competing priorities weighed heavily on me. I'd go to work and put my 'game face' on each day; but the exhaustion and doubt crashed down on me every evening when I got home.

At this time, senior executives at News International (the parent company of *The Times* which was later rebranded as News UK) could see the writing on the wall for newspaper revenue. They called together a small group of journalists to reinvent the future of the paper. I was a member of this group. This behemoth of a task turned into the development of *The Times* membership model and one of the biggest transformations the industry had seen. It would go on to be pivotal in supporting the newspaper to make a profit for the first time in 13 years, and it led the way for the entire industry. Of course, when we started out on the journey, we couldn't know that it would be successful.

The stakes were high. We were transforming a website that had, for the entirety of its existence, been completely free of charge, to putting a price tag on it. It was a fundamental re-imagining of the place of a news organisation in a market disrupted by Facebook and Google. *The Times* had to persuade readers, journalists, and commercial partners to come on board. It was a battle on every front – from creating the digital product itself, to evolving the culture and processes of a 250-year-old institution to become fit for the digital age. And no one had ever done it before. To say it was an invitation for me to step up and out of my comfort zone is something of an understatement. The responsibility was enormous. We were not only working to secure the future of the paper; it was also about securing the future of the industry. It was terrifying, and it was thrillingly exciting. Playing a part in leading through this disruption was an amazing experience while also being a direct challenge to much of my conditioning.

There would be no perfect solution, instead a good deal of experimenting and making mistakes along the way – so my perfectionism was on high alert. This transformation meant taking the organisation in a direction it deeply resisted, resulting in my people-pleasing tendencies being severely challenged. And it would never be 'done', meaning my drive to work, work, work until the task was completed was tested to its limit. Ultimately, facing into my own leadership patterns gave me insight into how we needed to work differently with others – the rest of the organisation, our customers, and partners – through that change. Navigating conflict and uncertainty were daily battles and it took an enormous amount of intellectual and emotional investment to steer the course. I was frequently spent. This experience made me deeply curious about how organisations transform: I was convinced that there must be a better way.

Understanding my purpose: transforming transformation

It is well-known that the majority of digital transformation efforts fail. Many change management practices were born of a post-industrial world: plan outcome A, implement steps 1–5: outcome achieved. This 'waterfall' approach can work well where conditions are relatively constant. But the tricky thing with digital is that it doesn't play by these rules. *The Times*' transformation was my training ground in leading through uncertainty. It taught me that the old way of 'managing change' simply doesn't work in the context of the volatile, uncertain, complex, ambiguous world of digital where the destination is rarely clear, and the path is not remotely linear. It also gave me deep insight into the importance of taking a more 'person-centred' approach to leading change. Day after day I witnessed the human impact of transformation – my teams' efforts to drive change through were often met with fear, anger, or apathy. This human toll of disruption was well described in the 1960s by Alvin Toffler as 'future shock' – a taxed psychological state of individuals and entire societies as a result of constant change.

It became clear to me that leading through uncertainty means paying attention to who I was 'being' as a leader as well as what I was 'doing'. I knew I had to become more conscious of my behaviour patterns in order to unlock my potential and that of others: I needed to learn how to work with those patterns rather than succumb to them or try to repress them. As I began this work on myself, I quickly came to realise that what I needed went well beyond another piece of intellectual development. I couldn't think my way to making the shift that I wanted, I had to work with my whole self so that I could begin to sense and feel the habitual patterns I'd embodied over time – the patterns that shaped my actions and interactions. Working somatically with Eunice as my coach I discovered what was really important to me as a leader and how my embodied habits and patterns limited my ability to step into the future I wanted to create for myself and others. I learned to turn my attention inwards, to reorganise my psychobiology so that I could show up differently and not be run by my reactive patterns but could consciously choose how I wanted to respond in the moment to any given situation. I was literally shifting my shape and over time and through practice my new shape became embodied – I could access the new behaviour I desired with ease. This unlocked more powerful relationships with those I worked with.

Developing my framework: digital is human

Being part of leading this change at *The Times*, combined with moving through my own leadership learning, helped me to create my framework for digital transformation. Taking a human-centred approach in the context of radical, relentless and unpredictable change is, I believe, the foundation of success. That means being attuned to the emotional, physical and mental landscape of the organisation and its people. Only then is it possible to enable others to harness their full creativity. I realised that it was these specific demands that organisations and leaders must find better answers to if they were to evolve and succeed.

I relished the challenges of business transformation. I continued to read voraciously about innovation cultures, human-centred design and agile practices and with my new-found confidence I was able to experiment and to practise new approaches. This was a real shift for me: previously I needed to have all the answers and know I'd got it right before moving to action. I borrowed from psychology and organisational culture theories and applied them in taking a systemic approach to organisational development. I trained as a coach, after being blown away by the power of coaching when I experienced it first-hand: I used coaching techniques in my day-to-day conversations. I mixed new potions by bringing together the ingredients of my embodied, authentic presence with asking powerful questions, listening beyond the words and holding my own ground, all the time practising new ways to connect and converse which allowed me to expand my impact as a leader. It was a time of rich discovery. I was excited by the possibility of this fresh approach.

Once again, I had a slow dawning that I was being called to spread my wings, to take this new way of doing things out into the world and to work with other industries that were facing disruption. In 2016, I was ready to make my next bold leap: I left *The Times* to set up my own business supporting leaders and teams to develop strategy and evolve their organisations towards new target operating models. It was a high-stake move. I was in my early 40s with a mortgage and three children. It was in the midst of economic and political uncertainty in the aftermath of the Brexit vote. But I had to take the risk. Once again, I was choosing to catapult myself into uncertainty: setting up my business was a moment when I needed to follow my soul's evolution – an evolution that has taken me deep into finding ways to quiet the voices of what I 'should' be doing, and tune into the innate wisdom of my inner pathfinder.

Riding the rollercoaster of being self-employed saw me navigate some familiar patterns again, but this time through fresh challenges, seeing my reactive tendencies anew. There were certainly moments of feeling lost. I may have been building more clarity about my purpose, but often those old patterns would show up, demanding my attention, particularly when I was in the grip of dealing with challenging psychodynamics in my clients' businesses. At times, I was caught in my overriding urge to paddle hard while maintaining a façade of calm. That 'work hard' ethic along with a sense that I have to be 'perfect' resulted in my heaping huge pressure on myself. However, I was able to dive into deep reflection, to tune into my body which has been the birthplace of finding new ways of being. I had to learn to trust others with my vulnerabilities. That's not been easy – seeking help means revealing to others that I'm struggling with something and my inner critic often responds with a shower of 'shoulds': 'you should know the answers'; 'you shouldn't be finding this difficult'. But gradually I've learned to open up to others more. I've built relationships with people I trust and with whom I can 'show up' with all my imperfections. I've invested in coaching and further work with Eunice by joining a small leadership group – using somatic practices to work through real-life challenges.

Remembering back to the first day I joined Eunice's action learning group back in 2016, I was struck by how embodied my sense of anxiety was. I began to notice how I carried that anxiety – both in my physical shape which was contracted and tense, and in my emotions which would be flooded with overwhelm as I worried about whether I could make my business work or whether I'd be 'good enough'. As I travelled deeper, I've developed rich insights into my presence and leadership. This has allowed me to slow down and become aware; by tuning into 'how I am' I have been able to work with my reactions and adjust them, so I'm not taken hostage by old patterns. When in the grip of overwhelm, centring has helped me tap into greater equanimity and unlocked deeper creativity and connection with others. I realise now how much the process of working 'through' rather than 'against' my patterns has opened up new possibilities, not just for me personally, but also in the work that I do with others. I understand the challenges many of my clients are working through because I've lived them myself.

I've learned that in working on myself, I can have greater capacity to 'choose' to be the most skilful version of me. I've also learned that by applying a human lens with the individuals and organisations I work with, I could have the most impact in helping them unlock their potential. Developing deeper self-awareness has enabled me to be more sophisticated in tuning into other people's patterns. This 'inward' focus has been pivotal to helping me grow as an individual and as a leader.

OK. Let's talk about power

Stepping into my power has meant following my instinct and following through in repeatedly taking risks, both large and small. Over and over again, stepping into my power has challenged me to look inwards and to overcome the fears that were triggered in me at each of these pivotal moments. I can now tune into what's really important to me. It's helped me decode what I was hard wired to do – to work through conditioning that has sometimes stood in my way, and instead identify the strengths and capabilities that have helped me be the best I can be.

Our belief systems are laid down during childhood, and for women, many of our biggest influences – upbringing, education, and societal mores – have given us messages that have encouraged us to please people, toe the line and 'be good'. When we decide to leave the safety of those confines, we can feel like we are in the wilderness – and yet we must face into our own fear patterns as we break the mould.

Exploring my strengths and limiting patterns gave me greater insight into the challenges other women face in an industry where they're not yet represented equally. Women hold just 15% of STEM (Science, Technology, Engineering and Mathematics) roles across the UK, and only 5% of leadership positions in the technology industry. Women's voices and perspectives are desperately needed: inclusive teams are essential in building digital products that respond to the diverse world they'll exist in, ensuring that they meet the needs of all groups. I wanted to create a space for women to show up authentically, and between 2016 and 2019, I was able to do that through my work as co-founder of 10 Digital Ladies, a networking group for more than 2,000 senior women.

10 Digital Ladies was first set up by a former colleague in 2013 – its aim was to create a space for women in the male-dominated world of digital. Our purpose was to enable women to have the conversations that truly mattered to them.

Whilst recognising that we couldn't change the whole system overnight, we were able to support women in cultivating their voice and recognising their power. We secured sponsorship and ran monthly events, an annual awards ceremony for more than

250 people in London and published blog posts from members of our network. In 2017 I decided to publish a book of *Career Hacks* crowd-sourced from our community – another steep learning curve and an achievement I'm very proud of!

The feedback we consistently got from our members was that our brand of open conversation and authentic networking simply hadn't existed before. We created the space to connect and talk about topics that so often remain unspoken: working with vulnerability, navigating imposter syndrome, finding our voice, discovering our purpose, building resilience and being supported in stepping into our power. It required me to 'put myself out there', share my own experiences; and while this can at times feel like a terrifying experience, seeing others respond so positively is deeply rewarding and I've gradually come to see the power of these open conversations.

My ongoing journey

Each time I've plucked up the courage to follow my instinct, it has led me closer and closer to what makes my soul soar. By following my heart's passions, I've been able to weave my path forwards. The intricate patterns of this process frequently only become visible with hindsight. But by following my wayfarers – my values and what makes me feel alive – the path has become clear, giving me clues as to what I needed to pay attention to as I build my future. This is what it means to me to step into my power.

As I continue to cultivate my leadership and develop my identity as a senior leader, I repeatedly encounter fresh challenges that can see me meeting my old friends of overwhelm, perfectionism and making myself small. Those patterns will never go away – this is what it is to be human. But through the work that I've done with Eunice and others – through somatic practices and creating space for authentic conversations and connection with others, by listening to my body, and compassionately tuning into what thoughts and feelings are triggered at times of challenge – I am able to be more choiceful, more skilful as a leader. This requires a constant practice. Yet in doing so I'm honouring my commitment to become me.

***

My 20-year career has seen me navigate the digital revolution on the frontline. Like many others in my generation, I've experienced the transition from the almost pre-historic, pre-digital period, to a world where AI will be replacing many of our jobs. This shift has brought about a fundamental disruption in the ways we communicate, socialise and work. But more crucially, it's caused a shift to constant, rapid change being the new normal.

I've experienced this journey as an individual seeking my purpose, as a practitioner seeking my profession and as a woman seeking to increase my impact in the world. My story has played out in many ways: it's one of personal development which has seen me 'step up' and increase my capacity to navigate complex change; it's one of professional development, leading major transformation in the newspaper industry, and setting up my own consulting and coaching business; and it's one of enabling other women to realise their true potential in an industry where they're a minority.

As I turn the page to open the next chapter, I do so with a deeper sense of self and the capacity to notice and interrupt my reactivity, to consciously choose how I want to respond, taking action aligned with what matters to me and my clients.

What the research revealed…

Research theme four: The power of tuning into the wisdom of the body, interrupting default patterns of response, re-organising in the moment, stepping into skilful action.

It was Viktor Frankl[43] who said, "Between stimulus and response there is a space, in that space is our power to choose our response. In our response lies our growth and our freedom." Our history becomes embodied and shapes the actions we want to take and the conversations we want to engage in. By tuning into the wisdom on the body, we can become aware of the physical sensations that are associated with our automatic, habitual patterns of response. Our capacity to sense into this hidden intelligence enables us to access that space Frankl talks about and in so doing we access more choice and an increased sense of possibility for ourselves. Many of the women leaders told stories of what became possible once they learnt how to notice and interrupt their automatic patterns of response which they described in different ways: "I make myself small", "I like to be liked so I hold myself back", "In that moment I don't want to be seen" or "I become a difficult woman, I become bullish."

The stories I heard evidenced a connection between noticing and interrupting our automatic habitual behaviour in the moment and our capacity to show up in our power.

Bojana Reiner, Associate Director at the European Bank of Reconstruction and Development (EBRD), shared her big learning when I worked with her when she attended the 'Stepping into the Power' programme we designed and delivered for EBRD; "Centring beforehand allows me to show up more confidently, more focused and more in control. When I centre in my power, I am able to adapt and respond to what is happening around me more skilfully, I can influence others and produce a particular result."

Rebecca Strickland, who at the time of the research was Head of Global Mobility, E.ON, told me that, "Through this learning and ongoing practice I can interrupt my habit of retreating. I can re-centre, feel my ground and access my power from within." This was echoed by a female entrepreneur who said, "I am growing in confidence to step into my own authorship, listening to the wisdom of my body."

A leader's ability to tune into her embodied state and self-regulate her automatic habitual responses in the moment increases her capacity to make the contribution that is uniquely hers to make.

An invitation to practise – My conditioned response

In this chapter, Lucia shared with us how she found herself caught in her reactivity. We all embody automatic conditioned responses; they're adaptive behaviours that we've developed in order to take care of our fundamental needs of safety, belonging and dignity. Alongside the familiar fight and flight, we also have freeze, appease and disassociate. These conditioned responses function in wise and adaptive ways, often beyond our conscious awareness or our capacity to control them.

Try this for yourself

Settle into a seated posture, let your breath drop so you're breathing from your belly, feel your back in your chair and your feet on the ground. See if you can recall a time when you felt triggered by something or someone, maybe it was an email landing in your inbox, a difficult conversation you found yourself in or a constant flow of demands, whatever it was, see if you can take yourself back there. As you recall the situation, notice what's happening in your body, notice your sensations in this present moment, notice temperature, pressure, what happens to your breath, where you feel taut or contracted. Notice if you have an immediate impetus to:

- Fight – push back or challenge.
- Flight – get out of the way, removing yourself from what's unfolding around you.
- Freeze – feel unable to move or speak, you go blank.
- Appease – make yourself smaller, avoiding any eye contact and maybe feeling the need to apologise or just agree.
- Disassociate – shrink inside of yourself, thinking of being in some other place other than where you are right now.

What did you notice?

What is your mood and what action is possible for you from this place?

As we become more aware of our physical response to being triggered, we get more familiar with our own patterning in a way that allows us to interrupt our automaticity. From awareness we then have choice; we can centre and respond more skilfully.

Remember, as you become more aware of your adaptive patterns, be compassionate with yourself as we've taken these on to take care of our safety, belonging and dignity. They're wise protective strategies and we want to hold them in that way.

I've known and worked with Amy Castoro for over 12 years. During that time, I've observed her relentless commitment to her own personal development. Amy recognises how her own journey of cultivation enabled her to step into her role as a CEO, leading authentically an organisation in a distinctly male-dominated sector.

Amy's chapter speaks to the power of working with the whole person, developing congruence between who we are being and the 'offer' we're bringing to the world. Amy reminds us that intelligence, hard work and awareness aren't sufficient to bring about change; we change through practice, and so she shares with us her daily practices that support her to take new and different actions and to have different, more effective conversations. Amy also talks about how she routinely tunes into herself in order that she might regulate her mood in the moment and choose how best to respond in the many difficult interactions she finds herself in. These daily practices enable Amy to truly own who she is as a female leader and to have a powerful voice in the field of family wealth management.

Chapter Six

Ladies, take a seat

Amy Castoro
The force behind soft skills

The founder of the company where I worked was training me to be his replacement and took me to a meeting with a long-time client. It was a highly regarded and exclusive private equity firm that deals with only the highest levels of family wealth, both domestically and internationally. We met in their upscale New York City (NYC) offices, where many of the deals published in *The Wall Street Journal* are done. At the end of the meeting, I asked where the ladies' room was. The conversation stopped cold, and nervous glances shifted among the men around the table. There wasn't one. Lucky for me, Roy, my boss and a former tackle for the National Football League (NFL), volunteered to stand outside the men's room while I went in.

That was in 2017. A bio break led to the astounding realization that all-male floors in the skyscrapers with the most exclusive addresses in NYC are still where many of the most powerful deals in the world are struck.

Now, as the CEO of the business, I see a huge opportunity to raise the voices of the female contingent in our client families. As women, we represent a growing force in the world. More of us are leading bigger organizations, generating and inheriting significant amounts of wealth, and moving into powerful political positions. Many women want their wealth to be a force for good in the world, their daughters to own their seats at the table and to speak from a position of knowledge about how a company's financials are driving its success or failure, as opposed to simply being a great team player supporting the (male) power centers of the organization.

My business enables ultra-high-net-worth families to transition their wealth and keep family relationships intact. Most of these families are led by men. The business was founded by Roy Williams, a man who was closely aligned with the traditional concerns of his male counterparts. After coming out of the NFL, Roy realized a lot of his peers weren't only losing their wealth but losing their families, too. They were falling victim to the 'shirtsleeves to shirtsleeves' adage, a global phenomenon that states wealth will not make it past the third generation. The theory is that the first generation builds the wealth without any changes to their value system. The second generation enjoys the fruits of their labor and lives a more upscale lifestyle with a different set of values. The third generation only knows abundance and, with little work experience, consumes the fortune.

The statistics indicate that 70% of the time, a family will lose control of its assets and will break apart by the third generation.[44] That's a staggering statistic. The very wellbeing of the family and the purpose of hard work are greatly at risk 70% of the time. Further, the cultural biases of men and women regarding money and power contribute to the forces that drive a family toward dissolution and lost fortunes.

More than half the time, the reason for strained relationships and loss of assets in families is a lack of trust and poor communication.[45] Talking about money is taboo in most families, and it also has a gender bias. In many families, still today, men control the finances. In a recent family I worked with, the husband made all the decisions regarding their investments. The wife, however, didn't trust her husband's decisions to make risky investments with the money earmarked for the family foundation. She believed the investments would fail and negatively impact her ability to be philanthropic. She was unwilling to raise this concern with her husband for fear of causing an argument or presuming to tell him how to run his investments, so she kept quiet. Her fear and resignation continued to build until finally they were spending more time on opposite US coasts.

In other examples, the husband may not be willing to tell his wife and children about the wealth transition plan because he's afraid they'll become entitled spendthrifts, unable to comprehend the plan, and/or derail their motivation. Often, we see the son selected for a position in the family business or chosen as the executor when, in fact, he's not the most inclined or well-equipped for the role. Often, sons are selected simply because of a familial and/or cultural belief that men are better than women at managing money.

Roughly 10% of the time, families break apart due to a lack of alignment in values and purpose of the family wealth. For example, the daughter who attends a top business school and is

109

deeply committed to the success and vision of the company is overlooked for leadership and/or ownership positions because she's a woman. Most often, the patriarch creates his vision for the wealth, along with orchestrating the estate plan, without consulting his wife, even though she'll likely outlive him and have to implement the plan. This creates limited, if any, buy-in to the estate plan. When the time comes to implement the plan, it's met with confusion, resentment and opportunistic estate attorneys. The conflict becomes palpable when the patriarch's lack of transparency collides with his wife's own concerns for raising children with broader, more socially-responsible values.

We provide families with the education and confidence that their hard-earned wealth will be preserved for generations and their families will remain intact during wealth transfer. In our family meetings, we meet the intersection of social and familial gender biases head-on. Challenging conversations such as how the distribution of wealth should occur, how the next generation might join the business or how to define the standards behind expectations and entitlement provide excellent opportunities to highlight the impact of the bias and invite new practices.

The social norms that lock women into limiting roles are loud and clear. For example, one patriarch introduced his son as a business owner. He went on to share how intelligent his son was and that he had a knack for systemic thinking. Of his two daughters, he described one as a great mom and the other as a bright personality who cleans out animal cages for a living. Neither of his daughters protested their father's description of their lives. The father explained his hope for his children: that they'll all get along and preserve his wealth. The difference is that he expected his son to make his own living. For his daughters, he just hopes they're happy. We then facilitated a conversation that invited the women to share their vision of their future, independent of their father's and husbands' expectations. One daughter revealed she dreams of owning an organic farm and raising cattle. The other spoke about going back to school to take her teaching career to the next level. Creating safety for these conversations opened new possibilities for the women in the family, along with funding options for them to attain their goals.

Mariko Chang supports this cultural belief. The author of *Shortchanged*, Mariko highlights a study of the wealth gap between men and women. In it, she states, "Girls, as they are growing up, are not socialized to feel that it's OK for them to have ambition about creating wealth, not the way it is for little boys. They're encouraged to take on roles that let them take care of other people."[46]

In the coming decades, the amount of wealth controlled by women will outpace that of men. We have some work to do to shift the way we organize women toward wealth and power. In the US, through inheritance, a minimum of $22 trillion in assets will shift to women. Forty-two per cent of top wealth holders in the US are women, including more than 3 million women with annual incomes greater than $550,000. This is a powerful trend that's reshaping the urgency and opportunity for women to impact their families, daughters and the world. And things are improving. Allianz Life recently updated its *Women, Money and Power* study[47] and the results are encouraging. More than half of US women are managing long-term savings and investments in their households, 37% are the primary breadwinners and 50% report they're the CFO of the family.

We're a largely female-run company; the CEO and the heads of operations, accounting and marketing are all women, and so we have an opportunity to tune into the concerns of women in our industry. When we run our family meetings, we always have a female coach in the room to listen for the females' perspective and support them in breaking the norms that may be holding them back from making a significant contribution to themselves, the family and their community. On a recent call, the matriarch of five sons found herself struggling to defend her vision of how the family wealth that she created will be passed to the next generation. Compelled by suicide and broken family relationships in her own family due to fighting over money, she refuses to pass the wealth to her children without proper training. Her eldest and most vocal son insists he receive a larger portion of the profits, refuses to attend family meetings unless they're on his terms and bullies her into agreement. Her role as a mother concerned with keeping the peace and being a caretaker and nurturer is in conflict with her role as the family leader being asked to hold her vision and invite others to fit into it, as opposed to her altering her vision to fit into their lives. It's no secret where we learn these behaviors: the messages are in theaters, advertisements and around our own dinner tables.

My mother's boots

It's late in the evening. I'm five years old, living in north-eastern US in a Victorian home with a wrap-around porch built in the late 1800s. My two older brothers are in bed and call me into their room to get something for them. "It's cold, and we don't want to get out of our warm covers," one of them explains. When

I walk in, they say "Don't turn on the light! It is in the middle of the floor, just a little to the left. Move back a bit… no, a little to the left"…and then *splat*! My bare feet hit a wet spot on the floor.

The dog had just had an accident in the middle of the floor, and the boys seized the opportunity to get some mileage out of the situation. Needless to say, I was barefoot and humiliated. It was a memorable moment in which I realized the cost of being in service at the cost of my own dignity. In figurative and literal terms, I could have simply turned the light on to make the task easier for myself instead of blindly being in service.

I ran out of the room crying, straight to my mother. Retaliation was swift. She rolled those boys out of bed and handed them a bucket and scrub brushes to clean the carpet at 9:00 p.m. – including all 20 stairs and the landing, clear to the first floor. They couldn't hold back their giggles as they scrubbed their way through penance. No shame, no guilt. Even today, the story is often recounted with a 'those rascals' coloring to it. I, too, smile as I reflect on how boys will be boys.

How often today do we as women accept the behavior of men with that same socially acceptable phrase?

When my father fell ill and could no longer work, my mother literally stepped up. She purchased a stylish pair of black riding boots, marched herself out into the New York winter and landed a job as the concierge of the New York Statler Hotel in NYC. She had four kids at home, and I was astounded. Her courage, range of diverse skills and sheer commitment to keep food on the table demonstrated the power of the female spirit in ways I'd never witnessed.

In fairness, those skills were always there; they'd just been hidden in acceptable social norms. She often pushed back and saw a better way. Early in our childhood, she saw practices in the church that gave her pause, and she pulled us all out without hesitation. Our front door was always open, our home a haven for neighbors who didn't fit the social register. She volunteered to write for the local newspaper, where she found a platform for her progressive views, hosted exquisite dinner parties that were the talk of the town and was fearless in pursuit of her own vision.

Once emboldened in her new role as head of the family, my mother blazed a trail for my sister and me, and she expanded the role of women for my two brothers to see. This role was completely against the path available to her as a child and young adult. While growing up, she did what girls were expected to do and wasn't given the opportunity for a college education like her brother. She was expected to get married. The cost of college was unjustified and irrelevant. I can recall standing in the kitchen one evening while she was cooking yet another meal for six people when she said, "Whatever you do, make sure you make enough money to live on your own." That moment changed my life. It was clear she had bigger visions for me and would be disappointed if I followed the path our society had laid out for women. She expected me to make choices based on my own career vision for my own life and made sure it stayed front and center. I saw my mother transfer her feminine qualities from the narrow river of social roles for women to leading and providing for a family of six.

There were moments when the edges of poverty were too close for comfort. I remember going to the grocery store with my mom and sister. We had a few items on the checkout counter: eggs, bread, milk and lipstick. The cashier said we had enough money for only three items. My sister and I looked at my mom to make the call. She said without hesitation, "Well, the lipstick is essential. We might as well be pretty and powerful." Her blind trust that it would all work out, her mantra of "Don't sweat the small stuff" (money was small stuff) and "This too shall pass" were the guideposts for my early training. I remember her saying, "Stay focused on what you are passionate about; the money will follow." And it did. Every month.

I still have those riding boots. I've grown the company wearing them as I march to business meetings with the same determination to provide for my family. Only today, I see the traditional female traits as a competitive advantage. I've stepped more firmly into my own power as a woman. I see that my wisdom and strong capacity for nurturing both make me a better listener. My highly-developed intuition allows me to make better decisions, and I have the humility to invite the voices of the rest of the team to be heard. These are invaluable assets.

Yet there are many instances when the social interpretation of my role as a woman knocks up against my ability to have a meaningful impact. In a recent conversation with a family, I learned the patriarch was unwilling to share the finances with his family because he felt a male facilitator could better understand and manage the conversation. In other words, he was saying women don't know anything about money and are not 'strong' enough to keep the rest of the family in line, so it was better not to have the discussion. As women, his daughters and I were unable to influence his decisions, effectively cutting out half the recommendations that could serve his vision.

Claiming our innate advantage

I face the clash of social norms and the trend of economic shifts in my professional and personal life every day. I second-guess myself when saying 'No'. I'm labelled as greedy when I don't accept a decline. I'm considered aggressive if I am too direct. My own subconscious sabotages my confidence with a relentless narrative of the 'imposter syndrome'. And all the time, I'm choosing between my own concerns and my historical shaping, which demands that I pay attention to the needs of others. It's a moment-to-moment struggle against the riptide of my social and cultural heritage.

My journey of breaking these chains and rethinking what it means to be a powerful woman continued when my brother began to suffer from a sensation of numbness in his feet. He was in his early thirties. My dad had passed away at age 57 after 20 years of suffering from an illness that began with a similar symptom. I was terrified by the thought of losing my brother from a horrendous disease of which little was understood. My brother met with several back surgeons, all of whom recommended surgery. With no guarantee of a positive outcome, he was willing to consider an alternative. I'd recently attended a conference at which I was introduced to the role of the body in managing stress, leadership, learning and every other aspect of what it means to be human. I convinced my brother to sign up for a workshop, assuring him that I, too, would attend in support of him.

During the workshop, I became impatient because the facilitator wasn't working with my brother. On the last day, I finally plucked up the courage to challenge him and asked when he was planning to engage with my brother. When he did, the

116

learning for me was profound. The facilitator asked my brother what happened to him physically when his wife delivered verbal attacks toward him. My brother stated that the muscles around his spine would tighten. Learning to release that tension was the answer to relieving the numbness in his feet. Without surgery. It was a profound moment for me to see the power of the body. I also saw the fruits of my courage for approaching the instructor and insisting he work with my brother.

A few hours later it was my turn. We were asked at the end of the workshop to write out our purpose. What was our own plan for the contribution we wanted to have in our own lives? I had nothing.

I realized that everything I did, thought and organized around was for others. I left the classroom in tears, shattered at the cold realization I didn't exist for myself. After some considerable coaching, I was able to find a way to merge my history as a woman into a powerful offer as a CEO with a clear vision to reduce violence in families. Through those conversations, I began to believe that my voice has merit, that my intelligence brings value and my determination to help others see their own brilliance is contagious. By catching myself when I stifled a contribution I had to offer, or not take a risk, I was able to tap into an inner reserve that was always there, just buried deep below the layers of socially acceptable behavior.

I made many mistakes, beat myself up when I failed and continually battled to remember who I was becoming. Through the tremendous support of my husband and colleagues and long walks in the woods, I was able to fortify my 'old self' that was always there and come home to a newly-awakened, whole self as a woman. The ongoing practice for me is to allow myself to more deeply internalize that my successes are due to my own efforts, as well as to those of others, and that I've earned the respect of the male-dominated families I work with – not because I'm nice, but because I've had a profound impact on their lives and families. I'm more rooted in my own sense of self and able to put that first, which allows me to make powerful requests, to decline, to question and to push back when needed.

Daily, I walk by myself in nature to remind me of my strength, re-centre my vision and experience the cycle of life. With each step, I walk into my own dignity and power. It requires mindfulness to make the walks intentional. A second practice I have is meditation. Sitting still and silent for ten to twenty minutes a day allows me to tap into a tremendous reservoir of acceptance, connection and kindness. A third practice is the regular conversations I have with my twenty-year-old daughter, who is finding her own identity inside our culture. The conversations are always an opportunity to listen for where she's holding herself back and where she can push back.

These practices enliven and resource me. They allow me to find serenity and trust in who I'm becoming. Reading books about powerful women and having conversations with other women who are committed to having an impact can rally me, even after a long, exhausting day. The unity and natural collaboration of women coming together as a force that contributes to a meaningful cause is deeply inspiring.

In my role as CEO, I'm often challenged. Recently, a vendor proposed to do some work for us on a consulting basis. I called to say that I thought his fee was too expensive. He was upset, believing his proposal was well thought-out and he had a lot to offer. For two days, I found myself feeling guilty that I'd offended him. Then I woke up. I countered his proposal on my terms and invited him to rework it so it was more affordable. In the past, I would have felt bad enough to never call him again!

Not long ago, I walked into a meeting. The client family members were seated around the table, but the seat at the head of the table was empty. It took me a moment to realize that I should sit at the head of the table, from where I could better facilitate the conversation and hold my role as CEO while meeting the expectation of my clients that the meeting would be productive.

As I face these daily decisions, I'm constantly aware of my childhood, learning to put others first. Now I see it not as an obligation, but as an opportunity to hold the vision of what I see is possible for them. When I show up as a leader, I can hold the intention and vision that allows The Williams Group to serve more families. Witnessing my own mother make this leap for the family I grew up with emboldens me. Having her as a role model shapes how I relate to my role as a CEO and to my daughter and son. When the tables turned at home and my dad was no longer able to put food on the table, my mother's vision and courage paved the way for all of us to survive and lead very successful lives.

My leadership as a CEO is focused on doing what's necessary for the good of the whole system, not simply on profitability. In those moments of facing what seems like a roadblock, my early shaping from watching my mother pursue her vision with unwavering determination shows up. I'm able to take a stand for what families want to have happen in their relationships, coach another woman to find her power in moments of resignation and design new offers that support my vision to build trust in families.

The historical shaping of women is very much apparent in the affluent families we serve. As I've mentioned, they're often reluctant to speak up in family meetings. When it comes to conflict, they'll frequently let it go and capitulate to keep the peace. Perhaps blind to the social construct that keeps them from speaking up, they don't volunteer for the positions that require interfacing with family advisors or joining the board. As a result, we typically see women side-lined, their expertise ignored. One such client built a very successful car dealership and spoke with pride about how his sons were running their respective divisions, the lessons they were learning and the hopes he had for them. His daughter, who graduated from a prestigious design school with an interior design degree, was relegated to the equivalent of moving the rubber trees around the showroom floor. Finally, in one meeting, we helped her find her voice. She asked if she could attend a board meeting. In that meeting, after listening closely, she simply asked when they were going to design a car that a woman would want to drive. At the time, the dad was planning his retirement, but the answer to that question has launched an entirely new line of cars. Retirement is nowhere in sight, and his daughter now attends every board meeting.

Stepping into my sovereign self

Having and *owning* aren't the same thing. I have the title of CEO. It's been a journey for me to own it. As a woman taking over a business formerly run by a man for the past 50 years, in a male-dominated industry, I find myself practicing the skill of being a powerful woman in nearly every conversation. I'll stop myself from volunteering to take something on and instead make a request or delegate the task. Often, women will volunteer without even having to be asked. I know, I used to be one of them.

Negotiating salaries with new employees, holding steady with my fees in a partnering agreement, co-designing terms of purchase-order contracts with large organizations and making the hard choice to fire someone are all activities that require me to be strong, clear and focused on my own vision for the good of the whole, as opposed to 'being liked' or putting others first. A key practice for me is to stay grounded in the questions, 'For the sake of what am I engaging in this dialogue or partnership? How will it allow me to take my own initiatives forward?' Asking myself these questions allows me to re-center on what's important to my commitment to keep our clients' family relationships strong and productive.

A second skill I've had to develop is how to let compliments in. Historically, I was trained to avoid being too proud, put others first and be the person who makes other people feel good about themselves. I recently asked a few of my mentors to share their assessments of me as a leader and coach. Their feedback landed on the surface for the first few times I read it. Then I took a deep breath, granted them the authority to make the assessments and allowed myself to believe them. This practice of acknowledging my skills, gifts and care for others has given me the courage to step boldly into new offers and challenging conversations. Dropping my shoulders, softening my diaphragm and relaxing my eyes to take in more peripheral vision create an opening for me to connect with my courage and growing identity. Feeling my feet on the ground and my back against the chair and letting go of my jaw drops my energy into a more grounded base from which to navigate.

Recently I was invited to speak at a highly revered conference as an expert in the field of wealth transfer. For a day and a half, I sat and looked at my nameplate that read 'Amy Castoro, President & CEO of The Williams Group.' I can understand this, read it, and write about it, but it's not until I know it in my body that I can really own it.

Perhaps the most difficult practice for me is simply slowing down. In my desire to serve, I've acted too quickly to take better care of the other person's agenda. Naturally high energy, I'm usually moving much faster than the people on my team and a few steps ahead of people in a conversation. Taking a moment to simply drop my breath and pause gives me an opportunity to check in with what's happening internally. When the external message is aligned with my internal message, I'm more confident that I'm heading in the right direction.

I now have the courage to go into meetings with highly successful men and trust myself to get the results I intend to. Without question, I live in the realization that I'm an equal, can go toe-to-toe with powerful men and reveal their blindness that's in the way of what they want most: building stronger relationships within their families. I'm confident they'll see a new future that wasn't available to them before I came into the room and begin to co-invent the structures and actions they need to take to achieve it. I'm willing to engage with them in situations of non-agreement and maintain a steady commitment and intention of producing an aligned understanding and path forward.

I'm inspired to materialize my own vision of what I see the market is calling for to enable us to stay relevant and continue to serve families and their businesses. For example, I see an opening to serve the next generation of family members to better navigate money and power, operate with more autonomy and trust the vision they have for themselves. I see another offer to support the patriarchs and matriarchs to find meaning and purpose as they turn toward the second half of their lives, in which amassing great wealth no longer holds the same appeal as it once did.

The company I run is no different. Having travelled my own path of stepping into my own power, I'm keenly aware of how the same social norms that repressed me for so long are active in the families we serve. Running a male-dominated business in a male-dominated industry has taught me to learn how men conduct business and to develop my own style of leadership and decision-making. I take my role as a female CEO seriously. I hold the responsibility of helping women see that their social training and talent are competitive advantages whose time has come. I support our female clients to step more boldly into their power, embrace their natural instincts and organizing principles of caring for others and turn it toward their own vision of what's possible. I encourage them to make their own footprint and contribute to their communities in powerful ways. I want their voices to be heard through action that merges their hearts and their power into impact. I want to see more possibilities than ever before. I want them to move beyond just being strong workers who climb the ladder by being team players to having the vision and depth of understanding of the financial and economic drivers to lead.

These same practices enable me the freedom and authority to lead the organization in new directions. While serving the needs of our clients and our team, I also claim the necessary personal ground needed to run the company responsibly. It requires having uncomfortable conversations at times – for example, when I must deny someone income. I lean on my history and remember the strength and boldness of my mother, who broke free of social norms and demonstrated a new model. Taking a leaf from Buckminster Fuller, a famous American systems theorist, "You never change things by fighting the existing reality. To change something, build a new model that makes the existing model obsolete."[48] As women, rather than try to change the old model, we're designing a new model that enables all of us to thrive.

What the research revealed…

Research theme five: The power of being in regular practices, cultivating the 'self' as the instrument through which you act and interact in the world.

Deepening our awareness of our embodied state gives us more choice, but this is only part of what enables us to lead from a place of power and authenticity: we also need to practise. We're already practising something, a way of being, it's just not conscious or helpful even. When we become more conscious of what we're practising, we can consciously choose to practise something different.

Taking on a new practice is a conscious choice that we make so we can behave and act in a particular way, enabling new behaviours to become embodied, or part of who we are. When we commit to a regular practice, we're re-wiring our nervous system, physically encoding new embodied patterns into our body which then enables us to access new behaviours with ease. It's practice that builds our capacity to reorganise ourselves in the moment, to return faster and more frequently to our embodied self. This is resilience.

In my conversations with women leaders they shared the practices they'd taken on and that they'd found valuable in enabling them to step into their power. "I centre before joining a meeting and re-centre throughout", "I start each day with a sitting practice so I can reconnect with what I care about", "I practise with my Jo (staff used in Aikido) each morning to remind myself to take up space", "I practise resourcing myself", "I practise saying 'no' and holding." Their stories revealed how through practice they begin to embody a more powerful way of being. They practise with intention, being conscious about the granularity of what's occurring in their body as they take new and different action. This, we can say, is the pathway to self-mastery.

Cultivating our way of being so we might step into our power is not instant, we're not learning a bit of information or reading a book to gain some knowledge, but rather it's more like learning to play an instrument; it requires the investment of time. But the reward is that by making a conscious choice to be in a regular practice it enables us to show up in a powerful way and become just who we are. Rachel Warwick, who at the time was Head of Talent, Development and Engagement for easyJet, said, "I can be more authentic, comfortable in who I am and what I am doing, I feel able to have more open and honest conversations and can collaborate more effectively."

When a leader learns to live more deeply inside herself, she can trust who she has become.

An invitation to practise –
Shifting the focus of our attention

As Amy shared with us, being the CEO of The Williams Group requires her to build the capacity to shift her focus of attention from herself, to her clients, to the context in which she is operating.

I was introduced to this practice during my training with Strozzi Institute and continue to find it valuable. The 'one, two, three practice'[49] is a way for me to experiment with shifting states from a narrow focus on myself, to a wider focus of attention to include those I interact with and then widening out further to the expand my attention to the environment.

You'll need to do this practice standing and you'll need a space behind you to step back as we move back and between the different states. As you move through the three states, notice what's revealed to you by tuning your attention inwards.

> As you stand, we'll call this state 'one space'. Here we're focusing on designing our present plan of action, what needs to be done, what we need to take care of. Let your attention be focused on you and what you need. Notice your sensations, notice where your breath is, notice your mood and your internal narrative that seems to arise automatically. Stay here for a few moments tuning into your body.
>
> Right behind you there's a bigger space which we'll call 'two space'. When you feel ready, take a step back into two space – let your attention drop, settling into yourself and feeling more width, feeling your connection to others. In this two space we're opening ourselves to

the perspectives of others, co-designing possibilities that may not have existed before. Stay for a few moments, tuning into your body.

Now step forward, back into one space and as you do narrow your attention back on you, bringing your attention closer in. Feel and notice what happens in your body, notice that automatic narrative that appears. Stay for a few moments.

Once again, step back into two space and once again expand your attention, widening your focus of attention to others. See what shifts in your body as you widen, what happens to your mood, your thoughts and your breath. Stay for a few moments.

And there's yet another bigger space behind us, what we'll call 'three space'. Take a step backwards and expand your attention to include the environment, the wider context, maybe even all of humanity if that feels relevant. Here we're listening to what wants to emerge from the rhythm of the greater mood and energy of this moment in time. As you expand your attention, notice what happens in your body, notice your sensations, notice your mood, your breath, your automatic internal narrative. What's this space like for you? Stay here for a few moments tuning into your body.

Step forward and move back into two space. We are bringing our attention closer in, to ourselves, to others, feeling our interdependence with those we interact with. Notice what happens as you back into two space.

Finally, come back to one space, bringing your attention closer in, to you, what you need to get done.

Notice what happens to you as you step back into one space.

Having experienced this practice, capture your reflections:

- What did you notice in your body in each of the states?
- What mood did you notice in each of the states?

In a world where we're more interconnected than ever before, I've found this practice is a way for me to learn centred interdependence, how do I show in each of these states, how do I act from each of these states? And what is the centred action I can take from each of these states?

You may choose to consciously practise this each day for a week, setting an intention for why you're practising and noticing what gets revealed.

Chapter Seven

Uncovering our authentic power

"It's time to stop trying to change women, and start changing the systems that prevent them from achieving their potential"[50]

UN Secretary-General António Guterres

Another call to action

The sun shines brightly this first morning back in Malta in the summer of 2019. There's something wonderful about being able to step out into the warmth of the sun, to see uninterrupted blue skies above and a sea glistening and transparent below. I'm heading into Valletta, on a bus crowded with commuters on their way to work, mums with small children and tourists embarking on a day of adventure. Transported back in time, surrounded by conversations – some in English, but most in Maltese, it's strangely comforting to be cocooned in a blanket of the familiar and of a time gone by.

As the bus makes its way along the narrow streets, my old school friend Lorna and I are in our own conversation, squealing with excitement each time we spot a familiar place or a building that triggers a memory, which is for much of the journey. We get off the bus just outside Valletta, by the landmark Tritons' Fountain which looms large in front of us, the centre piece of an impressive plaza, leading to the entrance of the city.

Walking across the bridge into the city, the modern and imposing Parliament House rises above the ruins of the old opera house, a visual reminder of the relationship between past, present and future. As Lorna and I continue to stroll down Republic Street, we're caught in stories of the past while being present to the moment, to the sights, sounds and smells all around us. Much has changed and much is still the same and yet we see it all with fresh eyes, as if we're seeing it for the first time.

We arrive in St George's Square. It was here I'd come as a student; it was here in front of the Palace of the Grandmaster, the then home of parliament, that students from across the island had stood in solidarity together, united in a cause, and like me, responded to a call for action. It was here that we brought our collective voice to stop something we all believed was fundamentally wrong. I didn't know it then but standing in that square, on a bright, sunny day many years later, it's clear to me; we had spoken truth to power. As a collective body, we'd not only found power from within ourselves, but by coming together we were creating collective action, our voices speaking with and for each other, and for others who weren't able to make the journey.

Standing in the square again gives me a greater appreciation of what we did that day. Looking back now, that early experience was my first lesson in the power of the collective, bringing the collective voice to invite a different conversation and to shift the system.

Fast forward and here I am writing a book about women finding their voice and stepping into their power, individually and collectively. It's a book that was calling to be written and despite my protestations, it was another call to action. And just like all those years ago, I felt compelled to respond, even though daring to bring my voice to the conversation about women leaders in the workplace triggered all of my historical conditioning; the deeply held fear that's hard wired in my system immediately coming to the surface. A fear that has me shrink away from being seen, afraid to speak up even when I knew what I wanted to say and felt I could contribute. The difference now all these years later is that I've come to know, at a deeper level, my historical conditioning and I've learnt to value what it's trying to take care of within me. No longer in a fight with myself? I'm able to notice how my fear shows up in my body, where I tense, where I numb and disconnect, alongside a narrative of self-doubt that appears unbidden and extremely persistent. In becoming familiar with how fear shows up in my body, I'm then able to soften, loosening those areas of tension and centre. In shifting my psychobiology, I'm able to access more choice, more agency, enabling me to step into what I feel is calling me forward.

The stories in this book all speak to the individual transformational journey each of the women authors have engaged in. They bear witness to how they've each moved beyond historical and social conditioning to find their voice

131

and speak their truth, taking action aligned with what they care about. However, if we are to move towards a more inclusive culture, which is what the world needs right now, then any work with women leaders must also invite our social system to shift and evolve. António Guterres highlights this in his speech to the UN[51], "Only through the equal participation of women can we benefit from the intelligence, experience and insights of all humanity." There's a need for us to move away from the harmful structures that pervade our lives, underpinning our society and our corporations negatively, something Caroline Criado Perez describes as "default man"[52] thinking, and to embrace a new paradigm of power. Bella Abzug, who was an American lawyer, a member of the US Congress and a leader of the women's movement, spoke to this when she said, "In the 21st century, women will change the nature of power rather than power changing the nature of women."[53] The time is now.

In this book, I've purposefully privileged women's voices, creating space for women to come together and tell their story of how they've been able to reclaim their power. By speaking up, speaking out and showing up for one another, women are changing the nature of power and challenging our 'default man' thinking. Through sharing their stories, each of these women has invited us into an exploration of power, courageously letting themselves be seen as they re-shaped themselves and their leadership to create the impact they want to have in the world.

Having read the stories, you may like to reflect on the following questions:

- What's been provoked in you by each of the stories?

- How have your own interpretation and 'stories' of power been challenged by what you've read?
- What does all this mean for you, what sense are you making of it, what questions are you holding for yourself and your relationship with power?

When we, as women, develop a new sense and interpretation of power for ourselves, we can transcend the historical and social forces that we swim in every day and bring our voices to shifting the prevailing culture.

In this last chapter we'll take a deeper dive into Stepping Into Your Power, exploring how it integrates different perspectives and theoretical frames with my experience of working with women leaders in organisations combined with action research. No two programmes are ever the same as I continually assess, learn and evolve through the work. More of this later in the chapter. I invite us to expand our enquiry as we explore what happens when women leaders from the same organisation come together to engage in work on themselves in the context of their system. We'll reflect on how their collective capacity to show up for themselves and for each other invites a shift in the organisation's dominant narrative, making space for new possibilities to emerge in how leadership is practised.

But first, back to the beginning, to how it all started. To what, at the time, seemed to be nothing more than a simple request from a client, which became a catalyst for another call to action: to develop a programme that aims to enable women leaders to access their authentic power while also inviting a shift towards a more inclusive workplace, with a move away from default male thinking.[54]

A powerful request

At the time, Håkan was the Head of Learning & Development North & East Europe for the energy company, E.ON. I'd worked in various business units within E.ON for about three years and in particular with Håkan's leadership team as well as with leaders from across the business. I'd grown to value and appreciate much about the organisation. Given the transformational challenges his leaders were facing, Håkan realised that they needed to deepen their capacity to build relationships with and across their eco-system, to manage their mood and engage with the mood of others through authentic conversation. The work we did was not just about raising awareness but also aimed to build leaders' capability to navigate and lead change while being firmly rooted in the context of their business. In other words, being the change they wanted to lead.

Having experienced the work for himself and observed what becomes possible through embodied learning, Håkan now turned his attention to the women's network, a group of high potential women leaders. He said to me, "I have an idea: how would it be to develop a programme for our network of women leaders, one that is based in embodied learning, enabling them to build their capacity to effectively lead in our current context which is uncertain, disruptive and continually changing?"

E.ON had pointed out a clear vision, making diversity one of the strategic initiatives. One of the key targets was to increase the number of female leaders in all levels of the organisation, mirroring the customer base. For example, they'd introduced a policy that in all management recruitments there should be one of each gender in the final three candidates. They also initiated a network of female talents and leaders to support this journey. The female network met regularly to learn and develop.

To support these strategic intentions, Håkan wanted to make a real step change for senior women working across the E.ON organisation in the Nordics. He was keen to ensure that senior women had the opportunity to bring their voices to leading the organisation through the demands of ongoing change. And that those women who wanted to put themselves forward to compete for board level roles alongside their male colleagues felt able and equipped to do so. His request was clear: Håkan wanted a programme that would enable women leaders to cultivate their leadership in context so they might *show up in their power*, thereby bringing more balance to the senior leadership and the board. He believed this would create a diversity of perspective that has been shown to increase productivity[55] and enable the organisation to effectively navigate the challenges ahead.

Offering a programme that placed the mind-body connection at the centre of the learning design would always be a stretch in a culture where the engineering mind was privileged. It takes a courageous leader to make such a move. But Håkan felt strongly that it was important for the women to come together, to learn together, to connect more deeply with themselves and with each other and to support each other on the journey and beyond. "I felt that including embodiment in our development activities added another dimension to my work that I had missed in earlier development activities. To bring it all to a holistic, somatic view connected me back to what I feel passionate about as a learning and development professional," said Håkan.

With a clear intention to improve gender balance at senior levels, I began to work with Håkan, and the women leaders themselves to design and shape a programme that supported E.ON's ambitions. The work resulted in a design for a six-month journey that invited participants to discover their authentic power through in-person workshops, one-to-one coaching and action inquiry groups.

As the women learnt to tune into themselves and what they really care about, they began to discover their true purpose as leaders. It's a purpose that's deeply felt at an emotional and physical level, manifesting in the quality of their presence. As they build their capacity to pay attention to their own inner state and their own automatic patterns, they become practised in self-regulating, enabling the women to access more choice in how to respond in the moment to whatever's happening around them. In short, they learn to show up differently and take action aligned with what they care about.

As a result of the work the women were able to come to a new relationship with themselves; one in which they value who they truly are, not just what they've been raised to believe, or societal expectations had created for them. They built a strong foundation for ongoing learning, a greater self-confidence and a deeper sense of awareness. I watched as they walked away taller, not physically taller you understand, but energetically taller, owning their dignity and feeling their value. They embodied confidence and a quality of presence that creates trust and invites others to follow.

Moreover, as they each connected inwards to themselves, a stronger connection began to happen between the women in the group. I saw how the more powerful one woman got, the more powerful every woman in the group got, each in support of the other, to realise their vision and what they care about.

This felt significant and I'll say more about this later in this chapter.

We know the impact and efficacy of the work, in part because of what we saw in the women themselves but also because we'd gathered data after the programme. We engaged in small group discussions together with a series of one-to-one exploratory conversations with each of the participants. We heard stories of how the women leaders were now realising their potential, no longer afraid to step up and step in, able to make a bigger contribution in their business areas. We saw similar shifts in practice with all the cohorts of women leaders who moved through the programme.

The request from Håkan opened a new possibility for me, something I'd not previously considered. I never set out to work with women exclusively, but I now felt a pull so strong it was impossible to ignore. I've had the privilege of coaching hundreds of women leaders. However, the work with Håkan informed the development of something different: a bespoke design that invites women leaders to transform by nurturing their leadership capacity inside of their own context, and by joining together in that process. 'Stepping Into Your Power' was born.

Stepping Into Your Power comes of age

Stepping Into Your Power grew out of the work I did with Håkan, it evolved in the context of my work with organisations, in conversation with them and through the action research with the participants themselves. Working in multiple contexts, with different global organisations, enabled me to continually distil and refine the design.

Stepping Into Your Power enables women to cultivate who they're being in their leadership, transforming their identity, determining for themselves how they show up at work and in life, thus massively increasing their impact.

Developed by Eunice Aquilina

Participants move through a journey of **awakening**, **transforming** and **empowering**; waking up to themselves, getting in touch with what's important and how they habitually sabotage themselves, transforming those unhelpful habits and patterns that hold women back, learning new ways of acting and interacting that empower them to show up differently.

Programmes are co-created with the client organisation, but all are shaped around four key elements that I've found to be imperative to any design. These are:

- **Including the body** as a place of learning and change
- Equal attention to how women are **being** in their leadership as well as what they're **doing**
- **A journey** rather than a single event, providing space for experimentation and purposeful practice
- An **integration** of the learning with the organisational system

Stepping Into Your Power weaves together the philosophy of language, complexity thinking, behavioural science and adult development. At its core, the programme draws on the ground-breaking work of Richard Strozzi-Heckler[56] in the field of somatics and embodied learning. I studied with Dr Strozzi-Heckler for more than a decade, becoming a somatic practitioner within the Strozzi Institute methodology[57]. It was a journey of awakening that enabled me to integrate all that I'd learnt and experienced with a more profound sense of self, deepening my capacity to work powerfully with others.

Strozzi somatics is a holistic change methodology that sees individual and collective transformation through a very different paradigm. The term somatics comes from the early Greek – *sómatikós* 'of the body', and which we can interpret as the living body in its wholeness. It sees humans as linguistic, historical, biological and social beings. We become who we become as a result of our interactions with experiences and with our environment. We embody a way of being that literally shapes our actions and our interactions, and these habitual patterns both open and close possibilities for us. Stepping Into Your Power works in the gap between what we currently embody and who we want to become, building our capacity to move beyond behaviours that hold us back and fulfil on what is important to us. Let's take a closer look.

Including the body – Somatics is the art of embodied transformation; a change methodology that supports us to embody a new way of being that's manifested in our capacity to take new actions aligned with what matters to us. With somatics at its heart, Stepping Into Your Power is an invitation to work with our interconnected self, our embodied self, privileging the body as a place of learning and change. When I talk about the body, I don't mean the body as a physical collection of tendons, bones and muscles, or the body as an image of beauty or an object. Neither am I talking about body language where our gestures may be interpreted by others in some way. Rather I invite you into a different understanding: thinking about the body as the sum total of our life experiences, a representation of our history, defining our way of being in the world, the person, the self we are. In this way we can say the self, our moods and emotions, our senses and our thinking are an interconnected whole.

This is contrary to the perspective held by the seventeenth century French philosopher, René Descartes, who advocated that the body is a collection of parts, a machine in service of the mind and rational thought. In this interpretation the thinking mind is seen as superior and all-important, encouraging us to distance ourselves from our emotional self and our lived experiences. Staci Haines[58], a thought leader in the field of somatics and trauma, calls on us to notice the impact of this Cartesian thinking and how "The mind-body split reifies a particular power-over system… who and what is associated with being rational – science, maleness, whiteness, education

and wealth – the 'right people' to decide, advance and rule."
In holding the mind and body as separate, it moves us away
from seeing the inner connectedness that exists in ourselves.
This historic split has created an objectified view of the body.
Embodied learning sees the body as our embodied thinking
and worldviews, it's our embodied habits, our ways of relating
and our actions. It's more than the body as an object, it's the
body as the whole embodied self; "to work somatically with
someone is to work with the unity of their being."[59]

As participants move through the phase of awakening, we
invite them to explore who they want to be and what they want
to move towards in their leadership. We ask the question 'what
is the identity you want to create for yourself?' These aren't
intellectual questions, not questions to analyse, but rather they're
questions to provoke a deeper inquiry. As participants begin to
awaken to the wisdom of the body, they also begin to wake up
to what really matters to them. These questions get answered
beneath our thinking self, they get answered by tuning into our
felt response in our soma. We get curious about what our deepest
self is asking of us: what is it that up until now we've dared not
to say? The body learns on 'yes', in other words we reorganise
ourselves towards a possibility. It's much harder for us to shift
habitual patterns if we don't have a vision to compel us forward.

When we imagine our vision for the future and feel into a
future that's compelling, we want to be able to express it in
language and speak it out loud, so it mobilises us. Dr Fernando
Flores, philosopher of communication and architect of the speech
acts,[60] who brings a special blend of philosophy, neuroscience,
and linguistics to his work, believes that language is generative,
action happens in language. We live in a conversational world

141

and through language we can generate possibilities. Through language, we can create our identity and co-ordinate our actions with others. Irrespective of our culture, all human speech consists of the distinctions of requests, offers, promises, assertions and declarations. Of interest to us here is the speech act, which Flores calls the 'declaration'. Flores suggests that through language, declarations generate a different reality, they open up possibility, shift context or initiate a new direction. A declaration is a commitment to a future possibility, a future way of being and when we declare the future we're moving towards, it fuels our intention to transform.

We should also remember that language is an embodied phenomenon; in other words the speech acts are embodied competencies. Our voice is produced through our vocal chords, our breath and the thought patterns of our brain. We can hear fear in a person's voice just as we can hear confidence or joy. The words we say aren't separate from the person we are. When we speak our purpose, embodying the words, we begin to *be* this new reality for ourselves.

My colleague Kate McGuire shares how she observed programme participants move from articulating a purpose statement to embodying what truly matters to them.

"We invite participants to craft a declaration and then offer them the opportunity to voice it aloud to the group. We stand in a circle and then one by one each person steps into the middle, takes a moment to centre and then speaks. And here's what typically happens:

A woman steps forward. Cautiously. That's understandable. They're presenting something of great personal significance, in public and out loud. So often their stepping-forward is tentative, apologetic. They don't make eye contact with the rest of the group; they make themselves small and narrow. They um and ah. They look up, or down – anywhere but at one of the other humans standing round them. They gasp a breath. They fidget. They preface their declaration with an apology or an excuse for its lack of polish or coherence or something else. They mutter their declaration. They scuttle back to their place in the circle. This is often the habitual pattern we see, magnified so there's no escaping the truth of it.

It's understandable, of course it is. Eunice and I, in doing our own development work, have both been there. We know exactly how exposing it feels. And we also know it doesn't produce confidence in the recipients of that not-yet-embodied purpose. There's a mismatch between the words they say and the message being given off by every cell in their body.

So as facilitators, we offer them an assessment, what we've seen and the impact it's had on us, and we invite them to begin again, to practise speaking from what they truly care about. We invite them to centre before stepping forward confidently into the centre of the circle. We remind them to re-centre and breathe, deep into their body, and connect with what matters to them. Feeling their feet on the ground and taking up their space they speak their commitment from centre, connecting to the passion they feel inside.

Wow, what a transformation. It's hard to describe the change in impact that comes from letting go of all those apologetic physical and verbal habits and allowing yourself to embody what you really care about. It's hard to believe how powerful it can be, how transformative, for individuals and organisations. But when you feel it in action, you cannot help but be moved by the experience. It's why doing this work is such a privilege. And it's why doing it in groups is so powerful, because it creates an army of witnesses to your personal growth who, because they've also experienced their own changes, become wholehearted supporters of each other, on the journey and when they all get back to work."

When we align our actions with our purpose, we have the confidence to take our leadership to the next level, enabling us to make an even bigger impact. For when we're truly aligned with ourselves, radical change is possible.

Being and Doing – As participants move through the phase of transforming they begin to reclaim their embodied selves, unlocking their capacity to move beyond habitual behaviours that subtly hold them back. Participants begin to see how *who* and *how* they are being is directly connected to *what* they're doing, and vice versa.

The quality of our 'being' is as crucial to how we show up in our leadership as is what we're doing. And yet we often put more attention on what we're doing, ignoring the person, the self who's taking action. It's working with ourselves as an integrated whole that makes an immediate difference to how women contribute in their workplace. The integration of being and doing is captured in the diagram below:

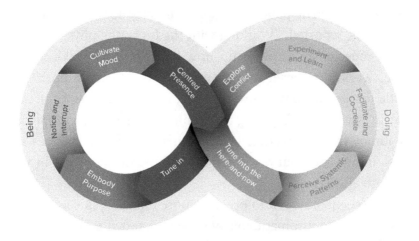

Developed by Eunice Aquilina

This ongoing dance between being and doing parallels the interconnectedness of what it means to be human, our embodied self. By continually cultivating our inner capacities we're able to bring our authentic selves to what we're doing in a way that creates the impact we desire. Stepping Into Your Power offers women the opportunity to develop and practise the art of tuning in to the inner self, understanding who they are as leaders, identifying their vision and building the capacity to self-regulate so they can show up more resourced and more choiceful. The diagram also highlights the leadership capabilities that I believe enable women to step into their power. In appendix three, you'll find a more detailed description of these practices.

We're the instruments through which we act: every action we take in our relational world is shaped by who we are. By focusing on who we're being, as well as what we're doing, we can turn ideas and aspirations into real behavioural change. As one of our participants, a regional director for an investment company, reported, "Working with the body, the physical, I am now consciously showing up in a different way. This actually does work; it is easier now for me not to get caught up in the little things but to be more strategic, meaning I have more of a say in what we are building here. Things are starting to happen." Without this connection to our inner selves, the changes we seek in our lives, our organisations and the world we live in will remain elusive.

I first encountered Jo practice more than 15 years ago when I started on my somatic journey. Being handed a Japanese oak staff, a Jo[61] as it's called, immediately piqued my curiosity. Just imagine yourself holding a 127 cm wooden staff in your hands, going through a series of moves and getting an immediate felt sense of what it's like to move with power. In just a few minutes, so much of my habitual self was revealed as I moved with the Jo. From that awareness I could practise something different, re-wiring my nervous system, *transforming* my habitual shape.

Introducing Jo practice to our women leaders during the in-person workshops is always met with a combination of excitement and trepidation. Excitement at the possibility of engaging in something that's very new and different but with some trepidation, after all it's a wooden staff. They begin by organising themselves into a series of semi-circles. They each stand with their left foot forward, holding their Jo upright in front of them, the base resting on the ground by their feet. We invite them to centre and then begin to practise the first few moves of the Jo.

As the women move together, they practise listening to each other in a different way, without words, tuning into each other as they move with purpose and intention. Inside of this, they're exploring their relationship with power, how they move with power and they begin to notice what's happening *in* them as they move together. Some consistently 'lean in' or overextend, losing their ground and almost toppling over in pursuit of making a move – straining to make the 'correct' move. Others seem to disappear, diminishing themselves with each transition. In their Jo practice the women are getting a felt sense of how they move with power, their habitual patterns, and who they're being in action is revealed both as individuals and as a collective. Indeed, they represent a microcosm of a living system and the collective shape they embody. By turning their attention inwards, tuning into their sensations, they begin to feel what's embodied in them. With careful facilitation we invite them to interrupt *in real time* their default patterns that show up unbidden as they move with power. By learning to shift their response in the moment and with practice, the women are able to build their capacity to own their power in a way that's both accessible and sustainable.

In the conversation that follows, the women begin to make sense of how their history, their default patterns as well as their relationship with power, is embodied. Working with the Jo, each woman is able to gain a deeper awareness that's unavailable through conversation alone. As those invisible habits become visible, the women practise new moves, new skills, transforming their way of acting and interacting in real time.

A journey – As human beings we're a collection of practices, we're incapable of not practising which means we're always practising something. As participants move through the phase of empowering, we invite them to notice what they're routinely practising, what's habitual and how is what they're practising aligned with what they care about. We invite participants to engage in purposeful practice[62]. This is important because while awareness creates choice, it is ongoing practice that builds our capacity, it is ongoing practice that supports the new way of being, the new behaviours to become embodied. In other words empowering women to *be* the change they envision for themselves.

By purposeful practice, I mean engaging in practice that's aligned to who we want to become, a practice that's felt in our soma and that's repeatable over time. It's through purposeful practice that the change shows up in our actions and interactions, shaping our leadership identity and how others see us.

A participant from the E.ON programme, Mihaela Cazacu (Deputy General Director for Power Operations), held a commitment to develop her team. She wanted to create an environment for the team where members feel able to engage authentically with each other, are able to tune with each other and can be productive together. However, her part of the business was facing some significant challenges, leaving some members of her team living in a mood of resignation, pre-disposing them to see things negatively. Others were in a mood of overwhelm which limited their capacity to see beyond what was in front of them. And others found themselves in a mood of anxiety which inhibited them from trying something new or different for fear of getting it wrong. Knowing our prevailing mood either opens or closes possibilities, the focus was on how to shift the team members' unproductive moods.

At the beginning of the programme Mihaela told me, "I am not well practised at observing my feelings nor the sensations

148

in my body. I am more comfortable observing the facts but the challenges in my team are not about facts. I feel I have much to learn."

Shifting our mood begins with awareness, turning our attention inwards, tuning into our sensations and noticing how our mood lives in our physical shape. We become aware of how we hold our shoulders up around our ears, that our jaw is tight, our breathing is shallow and high in our chest. This physical discomfort becomes so demanding that we feel compelled to take action to relieve the tension in our body. We find ourselves caught in our automatic, knee-jerk reactions of flight, fight, freeze or appease. By becoming aware of what we're feeling in those difficult moments, we can interrupt our automatic response pattern and open up the possibility for us to respond from a more conscious state, creating the outcome we seek.

As we moved through the programme, Mihaela practised noticing her mood and how it lived in her body, exploring 'what am I feeling about this? What sensations am I noticing in my body?' Over time and with practice she began to notice not just her own feelings. She became more attuned to how other people might be feeling. Mihaela practised centring in relationship with fellow participants, extending her energy towards others in a way that allowed a deeper connection.

Returning to the workplace Mihaela wanted to deepen the connections between team members. She was keen for them to process how they were feeling through conversation.

"I didn't want it to be me just telling them, so at my next team meeting, I had us sitting in a circle. We began by centring together and sharing our mood. I invited each team member to openly talk about how they were feeling and to share any concerns they had. This resulted in us having a really open conversation about how our negativity disrupts our co-ordination with each other. 'Hey, we feel we are together, we are all in this together,' my team members told me afterwards."

Mihaela could see that by holding the space for the conversation that mattered their identity as a team was beginning to shift.

This new way of being was not without challenge for Mihaela: "Sharing my own feelings and concerns, being so open was challenging for me and I had to centre and re-centre myself so I did not become defensive. I am really content about these meetings and how through practice we can change our negative attitudes to feel more positive together."

Our psychobiology embodies the action we habitually take, when we shift our psychobiology we shift the self and we shift the action possible. By Mihaela embodying her authentic self, becoming the leader she wanted to be, she was able to hold a bigger space for her team and to respond to whatever was unfolding in the moment. Moreover, as she continued to change, she became an invitation for her team to show up differently too. And they did; Mihaela felt they became more genuine with each other and as a result their collective mood shifted, creating the possibility for different action, both as individuals and as a team.

Moods and emotions live in our body, as does our capacity to build authentic relationships, cultivate trust and co-ordinate effectively. Through purposeful practice Mihaela was able to relate in a different way with her team and sustain that difference despite being under constant pressures with the business.

Integration – While Stepping Into Your Power invites women to work on themselves, to cultivate who they're being in their leadership, it's *always* in the context of their organisational system. As human beings, our body is a system. By learning to tune into our inner selves, we develop our perceptive skills in a way that allows us to listen more deeply to the wider system. This is important as I've come to realise that we need to know how to respond to what the world may be asking for, even if the world doesn't know how to ask for it yet. This invites us to develop our capacity to trust that what's needed is often revealed through what we see happening around us. Throughout Stepping Into Your Power, we help our women to develop this capacity.

Throughout the journey, participants work in smaller groups or, as I call them, Power Circles. It's a space where they can explore the challenges and opportunities they each face as a leader, where they can be coached and learn from their peers who'll also hold them accountable for taking new action. Being in this more intimate and collaborative space promotes care for each other and builds towards ongoing peer learning. (See appendix two for more information on power circles.)

During the workshops, we work in with the here-and-now experience, noticing what gets revealed inside of the dynamics in the group. It's also a place to practise something different and to notice how the self is showing up inside of that experiment. We hold that what happens in space, happens in life, in other words what plays out in the room, in the group, is likely to play out in the workplace, inside of the organisational system. By using the in-the-moment lived experience, the participants learn how to sense into the system in the room, paying attention to themselves, their own patterns, while simultaneously tuning into their felt sense of what is unfolding around them, in the different relationship and in the wider system.

In this way, the women build their capacity to notice the collective patterns that are embodied in the system while also paying attention to what's seeking to emerge that's yet unspoken. Women begin to discern the skilful moves they can make to navigate their eco-system. At the same time, by showing up differently, building stronger connections and having different conversations the women are inviting the system to shift too. Let's take a closer look.

Shifting the dominant narrative

In each of the Stepping Into Your Power programmes, I observed how the more powerful one woman became, the more powerful every woman became, and the group as a whole. As they individually changed, as their individual shape shifted, so too their collective shape changed. By shape, I mean our embodied way of being, the way we act and interact, our emotional range and the way we see the world. As their shape shifted, they more fully occupied their '*vertical line*', embodying their dignity and self-worth. They occupied their '*width*', energetically taking their space, becoming more connected and responsive to themselves and to each other. They were connected to an inner purpose and embodied a different narrative; this is who we want to be in our leadership, this is what we want more of, want less of. And because of their shared experience, they developed a strong commitment to each other.

As they each returned to the workplace, they became allies and critical friends, supporting each other as they moved back into their everyday leadership. They became practice partners, reminding each other to remember their practices and to show up in a way that was different to what was habitual, encouraging each other to experiment with showing up consciously. In this way they expanded each other's learning in context.

During the programme, they developed practices that enabled them to embody their authentic power, enabling them to show up with more authority. As a result, they had greater capacity to be with conflict, being able to self-regulate in the moment, enabling them to hold different perspectives with ease. This capacity to self-regulate enabled them to face into the inevitable resistance, responding from a more resourced, confident self, rather than from their default, reactive, historical patterns which moved them into avoidance, appeasing or simply pushing back hard.

The evidence from Håkan was clear: "I have seen a number of our women leaders embodying their potential and successfully moving into executive and board level roles. They not only embody the capacity to meet the changing needs of the business, but also now have a wider influence on the leadership culture."

We cannot shift the system if we don't expand our own individual consciousness. In showing up differently, the women opened the possibility for new and different conversations to happen. No longer afraid to speak their truth, they began to engage in different conversations, conversations that spark something different, conversations that further the greater purpose and cease to perpetuate the same organisational limiting patterns. This is not just about giving women a voice but is a collective energetic pull towards doing things differently, which may invite a shift in others. While only an invitation, it was an important one as it had the potential to stimulate some to reflect on how they're showing up in their actions and interactions.

Ralph Stacey,[63] an eminent thinker in the field of how the principles of complexity science can illuminate human behaviour, reminds us, "...organisations become what they become in the local interaction of people... from which emerges a population wide pattern." Shifting how the conversations and interactions between individuals happen opens the possibility for new patterns to form in the wider system. Caryn Vanstone, another thought leader in the field of complexity, echoes Stacey's views when she says that complexity thinking invites us to see how the possibility of changing patterns of conversations at the local level may amplify into a shift in pattern at the larger scale.[64]

I often liken this movement to the image of a water droplet: as a water droplet hits the water, it creates a series of ripples that expand outwards. In a similar way these different conversations and interactions produce the equivalent of their own *water droplets*, creating small ripples of change each spiralling wider with the potential to knock into each other and create a bigger disturbance to the dominant patterns.

Impactful though these shifts in practice are, they may not be visible to everyone. The power of these shifts can be enhanced and made more visible by us finding ways collectively to notice and talk about them. By creating the intention to notice, and having conversations about how the patterns of interaction are changing and what's happening as a result, we can magnify and amplify the 'disturbance'. Thus those small ripples of change begin to open a space for new practices that expand beyond the women themselves. As these new ways of interacting and conversation get picked up more and more, they connect in ways we cannot imagine, sustaining an ever-expanding shift in power. As the author of the highly acclaimed book, *Changing Conversations in Organizations*, Professor Patricia Shaw[65] advocates when we change how we have conversations in organisations, we potentially change the culture.

A move towards a more inclusive culture, away from default male thinking,[66] is not a linear process, it's not just about changing the policies and procedures or rolling out unconscious bias training, although that helps. It's far more organic, it's about shifting the conversations and how leadership is being practised and embodied, individually and collectively. Organisations are products of their leaders, the sum total of what they're practising, their every-day actions and interactions that have become habitual or on automatic pilot. Within an organisational context, what we practise doesn't exist in isolation, but rather in relationships with others. We're social beings, interdependent, each with our own needs, intentions and concerns. When we work together, it's an ongoing process of negotiation and exchange. It's inside of this human dynamic that a group-wide pattern emerges.

I experienced this first-hand when I was working at the BBC. You may remember I spoke about the 'Making it Happen' culture change programme in chapter one. It was back in 2002, when Greg Dyke, then Director General, laid out his intention to create a BBC that would continue to have relevance, purpose and public support among audiences and employees, far into the 21st Century[67]. With the support of OD thought leader Mee Yan Cheung-Judge, the BBC set about engaging 17,000 employees in many and varied conversations to collectively shape a future aligned to the articulated intention. The adopted approach of appreciative inquiry[68] in itself disturbed many of the norms and practices of the

Corporation and opened the possibility for something different to unfold. I observed how these new and different conversations seemed to unleash an energy that enabled the organisational system to connect with its own resources and capacity to change itself. This wasn't a top-down change but a change where shifts in the conversations and the interactions were like little fires of change burning across the organisation that had the potential to join up creating a systemic movement towards the desired intention. The change gained its own momentum, with even the most cynical becoming advocates for it. Through people's collaboration and participation, Making it Happen generated 2,100 ideas. Some 700 of these were implemented across the Corporation, improving the working environment for many employees. And perhaps more importantly, the BBC saw tangible improvements in its audience ratings too. Often known for its resistance to change, the BBC began to transform in ways we could never have imagined.

Taking a wider lens, we can see this approach to change happening in our society in current times. Think for a moment about the #MeToo movement. Originally started by Tarana Burke in 2006, it finally gained traction when two *New York Times* reporters, Jodi Kantor and Megan Twohey, courageously took a stand for what mattered to them by speaking up and telling the story of actors abused by Harvey Weinstein. By telling these stories they inspired others to find their courage, to speak their truth. Even though for most, speaking their truth was hard, not least because their identity was at stake, they stepped up and stepped in. As the power of the collective voices grew and gained momentum, change began to unfold, with new and different conversations about women in the workplace invited. Or think about the Swedish schoolgirl Greta Thunberg who couldn't have imagined how her simple act of sitting outside the Swedish Parliament every Friday afternoon would be picked up by so many, inspiring school children and adults alike from across the world to bring their voices to conversations about the challenges of climate change.

Organisational change is not so different from social movement particularly in an increasingly uncertain, disruptive and complex corporate world. I believe there's much we can learn from the social movement literature and research. In their HBR article, 'Changing Company Culture Requires a Movement, Not a Mandate',[69] the authors advocate that it's through a movement that culture change happens, rather than through a top-down mandate. A movement that often starts with an intention that's picked up, creating small local shifts that are subsequently noticed, amplified and potentially sustained.

Individual and collective transformation are interdependent and inseparable. You can't have one without the other. As women reclaim their whole selves, deepen their connections, embrace vulnerability and foster trust we become a powerful force for change.

In closing

As we draw our enquiry to a close, reflect on this question: What has us, as intelligent, capable women, continue to sabotage ourselves? My own experience tells me that while we may tell ourselves we must show up more powerfully in the workplace, when the moment arises, we so often fall back into our habitual self. I may commit to face into a difficult conversation, to speak up or even take a stand for something I care about, but then when the moment comes, I shrink away, I over effort or I lose myself. Sound familiar?

What my own journey has taught me is that we cannot think our way to being different, or simply articulate a new way to act, it takes practice, regular practice. It means disrupting our embodied patterns that keep us locked in automatic reactions and taking on new practices that help us to show up as our true selves. Each of the stories bear witness to this. How by stepping into very personal work we have been able to dismantle the internal barriers that maintain the status quo and begin to access our innate power.

I hold an intention for a world where, as women, we are all able to show up in the fullness of our humanity and embody our authentic power. It is a call to action, one that invites all of us, I include myself here, to operate from our deeper, more conscious self so we can make the contribution that is only ours to make. What is your call to action?

Writing this book is part of my contribution in enabling women to step into their power. It has invited me into my own enquiry, a journey of deep inner work, of discovery, of learning, cultivating myself as I continue to learn in and from my own practice as well as from each of the women, who so bravely contributed their stories. I believe that when, as women we develop a new sense and interpretation of power for ourselves, we can transcend the historical and social forces that we swim in every day and bring our voices to shifting the prevailing culture.

This is a book for women, about women, by women. A collective endeavour that asked each of us to drop our breath, let go of ego and connect to our deeper wisdom, letting our more conscious selves guide us to enable us to come together to serve a bigger purpose: that of 'stepping into your power'.

About the author and fellow scribes

Dr Eunice Aquilina

Eunice's work is inspired by her own journey, learning to be present to the inner voice of wisdom and in that, finding the courage to step into her power. She's passionate about co-creating spaces where women can come together in an authentic way, focus their attention inwards and discover a deeper sense of purpose: a place  where they can move beyond their history, find their voice and step into the contribution they want to make in the world.

In her work with women, Eunice brings a unique combination of experience, research and insight drawn from three decades of working in and with global organisations, building leaders' capacity to navigate change. A business psychologist, consultant and coach, Eunice has met and studied with some of today's thought leaders in the field of leadership and change. She has been studying embodied transformation for more than 15 years and is a certified somatic coach with Strozzi Institute. Eunice holds an MSc in Organisational Behaviour and her doctoral research explored how coaching conversations supported learning and change at the BBC. Her first book, *Embodying Authenticity: a somatic path to transforming self, team and organisation*, was published in 2017. She's also written a number of articles as well as contributing chapters to books on coaching and supervision.

Fellow scribes

Fernanda Lopes Larsen

Fernanda is a 46-year-old Brazilian-British executive, with a career in procurement and supply chain spanning more than 18 years. She holds a Bachelor Degree in Civil Engineering from the State University of Campinas (UNICAMP), Brazil, a MSc in Civil Engineering from the Technical University of Graz, Austria, in addition to a specialisation in corporate innovation from the Stanford Graduate School of Business, US. Her passions are documentary movies, learning new languages and travelling the world to meet new cultures. But her biggest passion in life are her twins – Maya and Nathan – who she claims are the reason for her being obsessed about trying to create a better and fairer world.

She strives to accomplish that through active advocacy for gender and ethnic diversity in corporate environments, in particular in Scandinavia, where she currently resides. She has coached and mentored several women in business and believes that holding space and lifting each other up is the best way to resolve diversity issues in companies.

Carrie Birmingham

Carrie has more than 25 years of experience enabling change with individuals, teams and organisations. Her previous role was as HR director for News UK, where she led the HR teams for *The Times, Sunday Times, The Sun* and the advertising team during a period of significant turbulence. She has led the transformation work for large  multi-million-pound change programmes within printing and advertising.

As a consultant, Carrie specialises in supporting clients to resolve complex and messy problems. This has included coaching leaders who've been promoted to CEO, tackling dysfunctional boards, supporting culture change to enable a new strategy and partnering a COO where a founder was accused of sexual misconduct.

Carrie has a master's in organisation and people change, is a qualified coach, facilitator, constellations and gestalt practitioner, able to use diagnostic tools, an NLP business practitioner and CIPD registered.

Alison Lazerwitz

Alison has more than 25 years' experience with international legal issues, including leading compliance functions, and the development of international corporate integrity initiatives.

Alison began her career in Philadelphia, Pennsylvania, as a litigator with the law firm Duane Morris. She then worked in the in-house legal departments of ARAMARK and the Wood Company in the US, where she was the company's general counsel, reporting to the CEO and to the board of directors. In 2002 Alison left the US and spent nine years in Paris working for Sodexo, the international leader in outsourced services. Alison was first the chief legal officer for Sodexo and then the senior vice president for international development. In 2010, Alison joined Swarovski as executive vice president and general counsel.

Alison is a member of the board of directors of the Women's Network for a Sustainable Future. Alison's hobbies include exploring the countryside, different cultures, art, ballet, opera and food.

Lucia Adams

Lucia is a consultant and executive coach who specialises in business transformation. Working in partnership with top tier leaders in corporate organisations as well as business founders in small and medium sized businesses, Lucia supports executive teams to develop their strategy and organisation and respond to uncertainty.  Her clients span a diverse range of industries; her clients include Google, Twitter, *The Times*, and ustwo.

Lucia has been driving businesses transformation for over 20 years. At *The Times* she helped a 250-year-old institution navigate the most seismic disruption in media history to become a highly successful operation fit for the digital age.

She brings a 'human centred' approach combined with agile approaches to navigate disruption. Her work has seen clients boost employee engagement and behaviour change while delivering shifts in strategy and target operating model.

Lucia taught business transformation for a digital master's programme. A certified executive coach (EMCC); Agile Change Management and DevOps practitioner, Lucia also has a diploma in management studies from the University of Oxford.

Amy Castoro

Amy is the president and chief executive officer of The Williams Group, a family wealth coaching and consulting firm. For ten years Amy has specialised in empowering high net worth families and their businesses to build trust and communication, proactively prepare for wealth transfer, and align on values and mission.

Amy offers more than two decades of experience developing high performing teams, leadership competence, aligning ambition with purpose, and increasing satisfaction and productivity.

Her experience with The Walt Disney Company, Adecco Corporation and Grant Thornton Management Consulting provides Amy with a strong foundation of leadership in organisations, creating cultures that work, and developing succession plans.

Amy holds a Bachelor of Arts in Organizational Psychology from Adelphi University, Garden City New York. She is a Master Somatic Coach through the Strozzi Institute. Amy completed a three-year business course with Hecht and Associates which emphasised innovation and developing new offers. Amy is an accomplished author and keynote speaker. Her book, *Bridging Generations – Transitioning Family Wealth and Value for a Sustainable Legacy*, was published in 2017.

Key terms I've used in this book

Action inquiry helps us to become more authentic while developing ourselves in real time, in the midst of our day-to-day experiences. It goes beyond knowledge transfer and invites us to observe the 'self' or who we're being, moment-to-moment, in our daily lives. When we engage in the practice of action inquiry, we're building our capacity to simultaneously conduct inquiry as we engage in taking action and in so doing, we dramatically increase our self-awareness and the overall effectiveness of our actions.

Action research is a methodology, a process of inquiry, which works with questions and concerns from an ontological stance of being. The aim of action research is to improve what we do as practitioners by observing, reflecting and making sense of what we do and why we're doing it. In this way it creates theories of practice which can then be tested and validated. The emphasis of action research is on continuous iteration over time.

Armouring Wilhelm Reich, a student of Sigmund Freud, proposed the idea of armouring. Reich saw connections between the body and our consciousness. This notion of armouring shows up as a repeating pattern of horizontal banding that appears in different areas across the body. Armouring may be seen at the eyes, the jaw, the mouth, the throat, the chest, the diaphragm, the pelvis, thighs, calves and feet. These armouring bands prevent or reduce our capacity to feel our sensations and aliveness.

Blending is our capacity to walk in another's shoes, to connect with what matters to them and acknowledge them in a way that cultivates trust without losing ourselves or blindly complying. Blending isn't a rational, intellectual understanding but an embodied awareness that comes from our felt sense of the other's concerns.

Centring is a foundational practice. When we centre, we turn our attention inwards and collect ourselves in a certain way. It's an energetic state in which we are more present, more connected to ourselves, to reality and to others. When we're centred we can be open to possibilities, we can have more choice, more agency and are more able to move towards what truly matters to us.

Embodied practices are actions or interactions that we've been doing for so long they are automatic to us. We may have chosen to learn these, for example riding a bike, or developed them in response to our particular environment. What we routinely practise may or may not align with who we want to be and how we want to show up in the world. We can choose to take on new practices so we can behave and act in a particular way. Through repetition over time new behaviours become embodied, or part of who we are. We don't change through awareness alone; we change through practice. Through regular practice, we begin to re-wire our nervous system, physically encoding new embodied patterns into our body which then enables us to access new behaviours even when under pressure.

Jo kata is a sequence of movements using an oak staff from the Japanese martial art aikido. It consists of 31 moves. Jo practice allows us to explore our relationship with power, develop our capacity to be centred and grounded when moving powerfully in the world.

Muscle memory is the capacity to take a physical action automatically, without any need for conscious involvement or intervention. For example, once you've learned to ride a bike, your body doesn't forget how and you don't need to 'think' about how to ride the bike – you just ride it. We can also develop muscle memory for centring, so that when we need to centre, we can do it automatically, without having to think about it.

Psychobiology is the study of how the mind and the body work together and influence behaviour. It shifts us away from seeing the mind and body as separate to seeing the mind and body as an integrated whole.

Resilience is our inherent capacity to connect with and fully experience our aliveness, to come back from the difficulties and challenges that stress and distress us. Embodied learning sees resilience as our ability to shift ourselves from our automatic conditioned response to a place where we feel safe, connected and have a sense of agency.

Somatics is the art of embodied transformation, a way of cultivating ourselves that places the body at the heart of the learning. The body, or our soma, is the sum total of our history; our embodied thinking, habits and patterns, our world-view, our actions and interactions. Somatics refers to the whole embodied self.

Space of emergence is a term I first heard from Fernando Flores. It refers to widening the focus of possibilities. It is the unfolding of contingent events that reveal new possibilities not previously possible.

Vertical learning is a term coined by Sue Cook-Greuter which is about cultivating the person you are. This is transformational learning as opposed to horizontal development, which is about acquiring new skills, abilities and behaviours. Research shows that those who engage in vertical learning operate better in more complex environments.

Appendix One

Research methodology

In the course of my work with senior women, I engaged in an ongoing inquiry into the relationship between embodiment and women's capacity to lead powerfully and authentically. The inquiry is located within Action Research[70], a living theory which suggests, *"as we practise, we observe what we do and reflect on it. We make sense of what we are doing through researching it. We gather data and generate evidence to support our claims that we know what we are doing and why we are doing it (our theories of practice) and we test these knowledge claims for their validity through the critical feedback of others. These theories are our living theories"*[71]. Making sense of my work and how embodied learning enables women to step into their power was the question I was holding. With my focus being on the 'how', action research invites an open-ness to the continuous spiral of discovery, noticing and responding to what's emerging.

I was keen to discover how women leaders construct and reconstruct their relationship with power not just in the mind, but in their actions and ways of being, with the aim of generating greater understanding of how women leaders step into their power.

I drew on Co-ordinated Management of Meaning (CMM)[72] to make sense of the different stories. CMM pays attention to how we make sense of our experiences and assign meaning to our actions and interactions. The '*story*' is the primary form of this process and how we tell stories about our own individual and collective identity and the world around us. CMM invites us to go beyond seeing the story as just mere facts to seeing the patterns of what is and what's beginning to emerge.

In this inquiry, I was listening to women's stories, hearing how they made sense of what they were experiencing in their everyday leadership activities as they practised showing up in their power. Noticing and paying attention to what may be unspoken and asking questions to deepen the inquiry.

Using CMM, I mapped each of the stories, translating what I'd captured into a snake-like pattern so I could begin to access what was being constructed and reconstructed. Noticing what the women leaders focused their attention on, what they were privileging in their context and what became possible for them as a result, and the individual and collective shifts in practice.

The emphasis of action research is a continuous iteration over time as I evolve and develop my practice. This ongoing inquiry invites me to research the questions as they emerge. What I share in this book is a moment in time that's been revealed at this point. The research continues.

Stepping Into Your Power
– design architecture

Stepping Into Your Power works at the intersection between language (how and what you think), embodied learning (how you habitually behave) and new action (what's possible), enabling women leaders to transform their identity, determining for themselves how they show up at work and in life, thus massively increasing their impact.

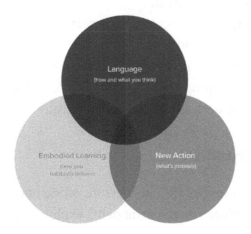

The programme design incorporates experiential learning, power circles, one- to-one coaching and if applicable the client's own digital learning platform. The journey is sequenced in such a way as to enable participants to move through the cycle of awakening, transforming, supporting and empowering women to move from their current shape and way of being to embodying a new shape. Through this journey, participants have the opportunity to experiment and learn what becomes possible for them when they practise something different. Through purposeful practice the learning becomes both self-generating and self-sustaining. In appendix two, you'll find a more detailed description of the programme.

Beginning the journey

We engage participants from the outset by inviting them into a one-to-one conversation with a facilitator/coach. The purpose is threefold:

1. To understand the challenges the women uniquely face in their context.
2. To begin the process of co-creation and working in the here-and-now.
3. To support the women to prepare for the journey ahead, inviting them to take accountability for their learning even before the journey really starts.

A living laboratory

We would describe the 'in-person workshops' as a living laboratory, a place where participants explore their relationship with power, deepening their awareness of how they've been shaped and how they show up from their current embodiment. Women work on their vision, the contribution they wish to make in the world and experiment with showing up in a way that aligns with the future they desire. Often that experimentation means engaging in movement practices, enabling the participants to observe themselves in real time; their automatic patterns get revealed.

They work in smaller groups to speak their emotional stories, sharing aspects of their lives that deeply shaped them. There are different forces at play, often invisible to us, that shape who we have become. By bringing these different experiences into our consciousness, we expand our way of seeing, making sense of what we've embodied over time. This is less about the group members getting to know each other's stories but rather an opportunity for us to learn how our conditioning lives in our body. And when that speaking of the story is witnessed by others in the group and by a facilitator who can listen beyond the words and notice what gets revealed, it's a moment of transformation. It's a moment when each woman, should they choose to, can step into their vulnerability and let their authentic selves be seen.

Over the course of the programme, women begin to learn to develop a new relationship with power. Through movement practices they begin to deepen their awareness of their current shape and their automatic habits and patterns. Equally, through movement practices they begin to experiment with new ways of being, laying down new neural pathways that open up the possibility for different action. Over time and through practice those new and different actions become embodied.

Power circles

Throughout the journey, participants work in smaller groups where they can engage in a conversation where they can each talk openly about what's going on for them in their everyday leadership. Members of the group become co-inquirers; listening, noticing what may be unspoken, offering assessments (feedback) and asking questions to deepen awareness.

Participating in power circles, the women begin to learn what's happening in the interactions between each other. They can notice in real time when they feel triggered or grabbed by someone in the group, or they find themselves feeling uncomfortable with how the conversation is unfolding. Women learn to work with whatever is arising in the here-and-now, building their capacity to perceive human systems. Power circles are a place for each woman to practise and to feel the support of other women as each group member practises showing up differently in the workplace.

Sitting practice

Sitting, training our attention, meditating, mindfulness practice, whatever way we choose to reference it, this most ancient of practices is increasing in popularity and part of any programme. We come into the world as inherently genuine and authentic human beings. Over time we layer on conditioning that generates those all too familiar automatic responses. When we practise sitting, we remove the veil that obscures our authentic self, opening up a channel for us to be in direct relationship with who we are.

A commitment to ongoing practice

It's worth reminding ourselves that awareness alone does not change behaviour; indeed the Astro tribe of Indonesia and Papua New Guinea has a beautiful saying: "Knowledge is only a rumour until it lives in the muscle." Therefore, it's not sufficient to be self-aware; to fully step into our power we must be able to take new and different action, to have different conversations, to manage our mood and to fulfil our intentions. Throughout the programme, and back in the workplace, women continuously support each other to practise something different. They're invested in each other's success, in seeing each other fulfil on their vision for the future.

Completing

Just as we attend to the beginning of the journey, so do we attend to its ending. We invite the women to explore their individual relationship with endings, what gets provoked in them and practising to stay present and grounded to the end.

Appendix Three

Stepping Into Your Power practices

"We are what we repeatedly do. Excellence, then, is not an act, but a habit"[73]

If we want to embody new skills, new behaviours, then we need to embody new practices. We've integrated internal capacities and external skills that combine to move beyond their historical and social conditioning, embodying a more conscious, authentic leadership that is sustainable.

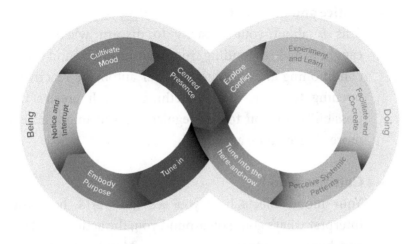

Developed by Eunice Aquilina

Being

- **Tune in**

  This is about your capacity to turn your attention inwards and tune into the life of the body and develop an embodied self-awareness. This is a whole-body sensory process that involves your extended neuromuscular system, your deepest visceral sensations, and some of the most emotionally-oriented parts of your brain.

- **Embody purpose**

  This is about your capacity to feel into what you care about, what matters to you, the future calling you forward. Responding to what you feel called to bring to your leadership in a way that goes beyond an intellectual articulation of purpose, to the embodiment of it.

- **Notice and interrupt**

  This is about your capacity to discern when you're caught in and responding from your historical and social conditioning and to interrupt your automatic reactivity, opening the space for something new. It creates the possibility for you to self-regulate so you might access more choice, more agency.

- **Cultivate mood**

  Your mood affects how you see the world, how you interpret what's going on around you, the action you take and how you interact with others. Moods are the very background tone of your existence. Your prevailing mood will open or close possibilities. Your capacity to recognise your mood and how it shows up in your body enables you to manage your mood and shift unproductive moods.

- **Centred presence**

  Presence is a function of attention: your ability to have your attention fully focused on two things simultaneously – both your own experience and that of another/others (the person or people you are with). Being present to yourself is about your capacity to feel and connect with a wide range of sensations and emotions without being caught in your internal narratives. Through practice, you can learn to have your attention both on your own sensations and simultaneously on others. This attention is built through practice.

Doing

- **Take up your space**
  Honour what you care about, not apologising for who you are or being caught in your own automatic response to power. Taking action aligned with your purpose, making a bigger contribution to the world, rather than playing small.

- **Speak your truth**
  Courage to speak up in such a way that you inspire and influence others to move with you. Claiming your space to bring your vision to life and make the contribution that's uniquely yours to make.

- **Make conscious choice**
  Hold boundaries for self and others, balancing saying 'no' with saying 'yes', making choices that align with what matters. Being able to feel a sense of agency.

- **Perceive systemic patterns**
  Tune into the patterns at play in the wider system, able to perceive the small moves that both strengthen and support your intention. Embrace conflict as a space of possibility.

- **Invite co-creation**
  Hold the space for people to process and make sense of what is emerging. Encourage people to work together, to experiment and learn.

Notes

Foreword

1   Moore, Suzanne (2020) Johnson and Cummings have revealed their flawed view of what strong leadership is https://www.theguardian.com/commentisfree/2020/may/25/johnson-and-cummings-have-revealed-their-flawed-view-of-what-strong-leadership-is
2   Anderson, Cami (2020) Why Do Women Leaders Make Such Good Leaders During COVID-19? https://www.forbes.com/sites/camianderson1/2020/04/19/why-do-women-make-such-good-leaders-during-covid-19/#68e29b4f42fc
3   https://thefrontierpost.com/how-jacinda-ardern-sets-a-new-global-benchmark-for-leadership-%E2%80%8B/

Introduction

4   https://www.theguardian.com/world/2019/apr/04/gender-pay-gap-figures-show-eight-in-10-uk-firms-pay-men-more-than-women
5   http://downloads.bbc.co.uk/aboutthebbc/reports/reports/gender-pay-gap-2019.pdf

181

6   https://www.businessinsider.com/wage-gap-gender-data-top-us-cities-2018-4?r=US&IR=T

7   https://www.mckinsey.com/business-functions/organization/our-insights/women-at-the-top-of-corporations-making-it-happen

8   https://www.catalyst.org/research/the-bottom-line-corporate-performance-and-womens-representation-on-boards/

9   https://www2.deloitte.com/us/en/pages/center-for-board-effectiveness/articles/missing-pieces-fortune-500-board-diversity-study-2018.html?id=us:2el:3pr:diversity:eng:boardef:011619

10 https://www.psychologytoday.com/gb/blog/wander-woman/201011/the-fine-art-female-assertiveness

11 https://www.bbc.co.uk/news/education-35419284

12 Ely, Robin J., Ibarra, Herminia, Kolb, Deborah. 'Taking Gender into Account: Theory and Design for Women's Leadership Development Programs' in Academy of Management Learning & Education, Volume 10, Number 3 September 2011 pp 473–493

13 https://www.bu.edu/today/2014/bu-research-riddle-reveals-the-depth-of-gender-bias/

14 Hegarty, P. 'How do we "other".' The Psychologist May 2019 pp 48–51

15 Criado-Perez, Caroline (2019) Invisible Women: Exposing Data Bias in a World Designed for Men, London: Vantage

16 Rowlands, Jo (1997) Questioning Empowerment Working with Women in Honduras, Oxford: Oxfam Press

17 https://www.theguardian.com/women-in-leadership/2014/sep/15/women-who-dont-help-other-women-myth-or-reality

18 Criado-Perez, Caroline (2019) Invisible Women: Exposing Data Bias in a World Designed for Men, London: Vantage

19 The methodology used to analyse the stories gathered can be found in appendix one

Chapter One: Becoming

20 Obama, M. (2018) Becoming, London: Penguin Random House

21 Rowlands, Jo (1997) Questioning Empowerment: Working with Women in Honduras, Oxford: Oxfam Press
22 Portas, Mary (2018) Work Like a Woman, London: Penguin
23 Cooperrider, D. & Srivastva, S. (2003) Appreciative Inquiry Handbook: The first in a series of AI workbooks for leaders of change, Bedford Heights, Oh: Lakeshore
24 Harrison, Roger (1995) A Consultant's Journey, London: McGraw Hill Education
25 Oliver, Mary (1994) DreamWork, Atlantic Monthly Press: New York City
26 https://www.forbes.com/sites/shelleyzalis/2019/03/06/power-of-the-pack-women-who-support-women-are-more-successful/amp/
27 Obama, M. (2018) Becoming, London: Penguin Random House

Chapter Two: Belonging

28 Wingard, E. (2005) 'Cultivating the Still Point' in Enlightened Power: How Women Are Transforming the Practice of Leadership, Couglin, L., Wingard E. & Holihan, K., San Francisco: Jossey-Bass
29 Haines, S.K. (2019) The Politics of Trauma, North Berkeley, USA: Atlantic Books

Chapter Three: Warrior spirit

30 https://artwriting.sva.edu/journal/post/will-new-york-invite-the-39-fearless-girl-39-statue-to-stay-on-wall-street
31 Representing the House of Commons, the Culture, Media & Sport committee is appointed to scrutinise matters within the industry. It conducted an investigation into the News of the World phone hacking scandal, which included televised interviews with key figures.
32 Parliamentary Report https://publications.parliament.uk/pa/cm201012/cmselect/cmcumeds/903/903i.pdf
33 Burch, N. https://en.wikipedia.org/wiki/Four_stages_of_competence

34 Clance, P. & Innes, S. (Fall 1978) 'The imposter phenomenon in high achieving women: Dynamics and therapeutic intervention', Psychotherapy: Theory, Research & Practice Journal 15(3) pp 241–247

35 http://www.aikidofaq.com/essays/warrior_spirit.html

36 Fairhurst, D. (2010) Words from the 'whys', Haymarket Business Media: London

37 Sandberg, S. (2013) Lean In, London: Random House Group

38 Cheung-Judge (2001) The Self as an Instrument, OD Practitioner, 33(3) pp 11–16

39 Tate, W. (2009) The Search for Leadership. An organisational perspective. Bridport: Triarchy Press

40 Bridges, W. (1980) Transitions, New York: Hachette Book Group

41 Heffernan, M. (2012) Wilful Blindness, London: Simon & Schuster

Chapter Five: Stepping into the unknown

42 Campbell, Joseph (1988) The Hero with a Thousand Faces, London: Fontana

43 Frankle, V. E. (2004) Man's Search for Meaning, London: Random House Group

Chapter Six: Ladies, take a seat

44 'The New Wealth of Nations', The Economist. June 16, 2001. https://www.economist.com/special-report/2001/06/16/the-new-wealth-of-nations

45 Williams, Roy and Castoro, Amy (2017) Bridging Generations— Transitioning Family Wealth and Values for a Sustainable Legacy, Oviedo, FL: HigherLife Publishing and Marketing

46 Chang, Mariko (2010) Shortchanged: Why Women Have Less Wealth and What Can Be Done About It, Oxford, UK: Oxford University Press

47 'The Allianz Women, Money, and Power Study: Empowered and Underserved', Allianz, 2016, https://www.allianzlife.com/-/media/files/allianz/documents/ent_1462_n.pdf

48 https://succeedfeed.com/r-buckminster-fuller-quotes/
49 Strozzi Institute Teacher Training Programme 2009–2012

Chapter Seven: Uncovering our authentic power

50 Guterres, António (2020) United Nations Secretary General 'Women and Power' https://www.youtube.com/watch?v=jH9DwGvnj2U

51 Guterres, António (2020) United Nations Secretary General 'Women and Power' https://www.youtube.com/watch?v=jH9DwGvnj2U

52 Criado-Perez, Caroline (2019) Invisible Women: Exposing Data Bias in a World Designed for Men, London: Vantage

53 Mitchel, P. (2005) 'Changing the Nature of Power' in Enlightened Power: How Women Are Transforming the Practice of Leadership, Couglin, L., Wingard, E. & Holiha, K., San Francisco: Jossey-Bass

54 Criado-Perez, Caroline (2019) Invisible Women: Exposing Data Bias in a World Designed for Men, London: Vantage

55 McKinsey & Co Delivering through Diversity (2018) https://www.mckinsey.com/business-functions/organization/our-insights/delivering-through-diversity

56 Strozzi-Heckler, R. (2014) The Art of Somatic Coaching: Embodying Skillful Action, Wisdom, and Compassion, Berkeley, USA: North Atlantic Books

57 Strozzi Institute Methodology – https://en.wikipedia.org/wiki/Strozzi_Institute

58 Haines, S.K. (2019) The Politics of Trauma, North Berkeley, USA: Atlantic Books

59 Strozzi-Heckler, R. (2014) The Art of Somatic Coaching: Embodying Skillful Action, Wisdom, and Compassion, Berkeley, CA: North Atlantic Books

60 Flores, F. (2012) Conversations for Action and Collected Essays: Instilling a Culture of Commitment in Working Relationships, North Charleston, South Carolina: CreateSpaceIndependent Publishing Platform

61 Jo is a wooden staff made from Japanese Oak approximately 1.27 metres in length and used in martial arts such as aikido.

62 Haines, S.K. (2019) The Politics of Trauma, North Berkeley, USA: Atlantic Books

63 Stacey, R.A. (2008) How Do Organisations Become What They Become? An interview with Ralph Stacey. https://youtu.be/RTAV7-FZLRs

64 Vanstone, Caryn (2007) 'Working from a Complexity Perspective Conversations with Caryn Vanstone (and Bill Critchley)' in Organisational Consulting: A Relational Perspective: Theories and Stories from the Field, South London: Middlesex University Press

65 Shaw, P. (2001) Changing Conversations in Organzations, London: Routledge

66 Criado-Perez, Caroline (2019) Invisible Women: Exposing Data Bias in a World Designed for Men, London: Vantage

67 Moss Kantor, R. & Raymond, D. (2005) British Broadcasting Corporation (B): Making it Happen, Harvard Business School: 9-303-076

68 Cheung-Judge, M.Y. (2006) 'Emergent Change Strategy at the BBC: Living AI During Client Contracting', in AI Practitioner May 2006 pp 27–33

69 Walker, B. & Soule, S.A. (2017) Changing Company Culture Requires a Movement, Not a mandate Harvard Business School Publishing June https://hbr.org/2017/06/changing-company-culture-requires-a-movement-not-a-mandate

Appendix one: Research methodology

70 Reason, P. & Bradbury, H. (2001) Handbook of Action Research: Participative Inquiry and Practice, London: Sage

71 Whitehead, J. & McNiff, J. (2006) Action Research: Living Theory, London: Sage

72 Barnett-Pearce W. (2004) Using CMM: The Co-Ordinated Management of Meaning, Pearce Associates. https://cmminstitute.org/wp-content/uploads/2018/03/16_The-Coordinated-Management-of-Meaning-chapter-2-2004.pdf

Appendix Three: Stepping Into Your Power practices

73 Durrent, W. (1991) The Story of Philosophy: The Lives and Opinions of the World's Greatest Philosophers, New York: Pocket Books

For exclusive discounts on Matador titles,
sign up to our occasional newsletter at
troubador.co.uk/bookshop

CPSIA information can be obtained
at www.ICGtesting.com
Printed in the USA
JSHW030509230922
30726JS00002B/8